Dreaming of the Dead

About the Author

Marilou Trask-Curtin is an author, playwright, and screen-writer. She and her husband still live in her childhood home in Upstate New York, where many of her spirit encounters occurred—and still do to this day. Her previous book is *In My Grandfather's House: A Catskill Journal*.

Please visit her website, at www.mariloutrask-curtin.com.

Dreaming

of the Dead

Personal Stories of Comfort and Hope

· Marilou Trask-Curtin ·

Llewellyn Publications
Woodbury, Minnesota

FIRST EDITION
First Printing, 2012

Book design by Donna Burch
Cover art © Wooden sign: iStockphoto.com / Marcus Lindström
         Oval picture frame: iStockphoto.com / Rouzes
         Vintage pictures with black corners: iStockphoto.com / subjug
         Floral background: iStockphoto.com / Peter Zelei
Cover design by Adrienne Zimiga
Interior photos provided by the author. Photo in oval picture frame is of author and her grandmother at a cemetery in 1955.

Llewellyn Publications is a registered trademark of Llewellyn Worldwide Ltd.

Library of Congress Cataloging-in-Publication Data
Trask-Curtin, Marilou, 1951–
  Dreaming of the dead : personal stories of comfort and hope / Marilou Trask-Curtin. — 1st ed.
    p. cm.
  ISBN 978-0-7387-3191-9
1. Spiritualism. 2. Dreams—Miscellanea. 3. Death—Miscellanea. I. Title.
BF1261.2.T74 2012
133.9—dc23

                2011045558

Llewellyn Publications
A Division of Llewellyn Worldwide Ltd.
2143 Wooddale Drive
Woodbury, MN 55125-2989
www.llewellyn.com

Printed in the United States of America

Dedication

As always, everything I write is dedicated to my beloved and much-missed grandparents, Edward and Myrtle McNally, who nurtured my dreams and my soul from infancy and beyond. Without my grandfather's acceptance of all things "ghostly," my mind might have been closed forever to such wonderful vistas. Thank you both for your love that transcends death and time.

To my wonderful husband, Dan—my champion and best friend in the whole world—I love you so much!

To our sweet cat, Pretty, who came into our lives at just the right time. Pretty spent a lot of time lying on my lap or shoulder while I worked on this book, offering intense purrs of encouragement.

To our constantly missed and loved-forever pets who await us in Heaven: Puss-in-Boots Cat, Midnight Cat, Bootsie Cat, Muffin Cat, Brutus Cat, Quincy Cat, Thomas J. Kat, Pixie Cat, Mandy Dog, Al Dog, Romeo Dog, Savannah Dog, Shy Boy Dog, Amy Dog—your nearness to us in spirit is such a blessing, and you have all proven that death does not destroy anything but the physical presence of your sweet furry selves. See you in paradise, my loves.

To Amy Glaser at Llewellyn, who believed in this book and in my dreams.

To Marqui, who took the time to put the flowers I sent on Butch's grave, thus bridging the gap from 1969 to 2011.

To Butch—who was my first true love. From the other side of life's door you continue to be my solace, my strength, and my protector. LUV you forever, Babe.

To my classmates at OHS for the info about our prom—was it really that long ago?

To my adopted mom, Anita: thank you for being there for me.

To all my "old" friends from the clinic: thank you for your constant love and support.

To all those who wonder and seek answers, to those who are facing their own mortality or that of a loved one or a sweet pet—it is my most sincere wish that this book will give you comfort and hope and a glimpse of Heaven.

Contents

Foreword

Why are we here and where are we going after we die?

The answer is both incredibly simple and unbelievably complex. In short, we're here to be ourselves fully, expressing the unique gifts, talents, and wisdom we carry—our contributions to the whole. And, equally important, we are here to love each other into doing the same.

I met author/screenwriter/playwright/public speaker Marilou Trask-Curtin by divine appointment. We look at the massive expanse of reality through similar eyes and from slightly different vantage points, as it should be. It takes each individual soul bringing through their own expression of reality to fulfill the totality of consciousness.

Marilou writes of maneuvering through dimensions to speak with those in non-physical form. This gifted author has breached the veil between states of being and returned with great good news of what is waiting there, and her message is delivered with lovely simplicity and heartfelt compassion.

Most spiritual orders speak of a version of Heaven, or nirvana—a place where there is peace, unconditional love, light, and no pain. Perhaps nirvana is a place. Even more, perhaps it is a condition—the condition of knowing oneself in totality as a soul, as a being of light, a part of the all-in-one consciousness and at the same time unique. Perhaps our overarching mission is to love into being the creation of Heaven on Earth. How? By bringing this awareness through to our incarnated state—bringing the beauty, the contentment of full awareness into physical form through our thoughts, emotions, words, dreams, and actions.

It is my sincere hope that this book will assist you in seeing the vastness of reality, in experiencing the magnificence of self, in building your own kingdom of awareness during your earthly life so that the next plane of existence you inhabit will be as Marilou describes: a place of joyful reunions, peace, health, light, and unconditional love.

Lauren Skye
Founder and Director
Inner Connection Institute and Church of Infinite Spirit
Denver, Colorado

Introduction

When someone we love dies, there is usually a deep yearning to reconnect with that person if even for a few moments. The reasons for wanting to reconnect are very personal but often have something to do with getting a chance to say goodbye, telling the deceased that we love them, seeking forgiveness, or just knowing that they are okay and that they have somehow arrived in that most beautiful of destinations—Heaven or paradise.

Such was the case with my beloved grandparents, Edward and Myrtle McNally, who both died when I was a teenager and within five months of one another. My grandparents raised me from infancy to age eighteen, and they were the most wonderful caretakers. They were full of timeless compassion, incredible wisdom, and a softness and kindness that put down enduring roots of love in my lonely soul. In fact, it was my grandfather who first introduced me to the realm of ghosts and that transition time known as death, and, as we shall see in a later chapter, he is the one I credit with helping my three-year-old self to embrace acceptance of ghosts, death, and dying as a natural occurrence and not something to fear.

And this was indeed a wonderful thing—especially when, after my grandparents died, they began paying me after-death visits in both form and dreams. And these visitations from my grandparents from beyond death's door seemed to open a pathway for me so that other beloved ones—and even a few historic figures—could visit me while I slept.

These dream visits from the dead have been both an incredible comfort and a deeply moving experience.

I know from personal experience that it is not at all easy to lose someone we cherish, be it parent, spouse, friend, or pet. In fact, it is an event quite devastating. We cry out for a connection to them. We long to hear their voice or feel their touch or know they are near. We yearn for them on such a deep soul level that we feel the tears and the sadness will never stop. In desperation many seek out mediums and psychics in a frantic attempt to coerce even the briefest of moments in the presence of the lost loved one.

Sadly, many of these attempts fall far short of what the seeker is looking for, and so the sense of loss and separation and grieving deepens and the pain continues. There often seems no way out of the anguish of the loss, and many people find their lives altered forever by a sadness that burdens their hearts and souls as they remain inconsolable.

Tears fall and the way back to happiness, joy, and normalcy seems a lifetime's journey away.

But there is hope and comfort, and that is what this book is about.

I suppose I am one of the fortunate ones because my departed loved ones began coming to me first in form when I was about four years old. By the time I was in my late teens, the dead began coming to me in my dreams. And through those dream visits I have had the unique and marvelous experience of being taken to the other side of life's doorway and catching a glimpse of the places where our loved ones reside and also what awaits us after we leave our earthly lives behind.

This then is my very personal story of those joyful contacts, and I share it with you, the reader, in hopes that it will comfort you on every level of your being so that you can find peace despite the loss of a beloved family member, friend, or even a very precious pet.

Death ends a life, not a relationship.

—MITCH ALBOM, OFTEN ATTRIBUTED TO ROBERT BENCHLEY

The dead have loved me since I was age three.
—MARILOU TRASK-CURTIN

chapter one

A Glimpse of Heaven

The Dreams

Everyone dreams, whether they recall their nightly forays into that realm or not—or at least that is what I learned years ago in a college psychology class. And during many of those dreams fantastic things happen. Some people report being able to fly; others ride a magnificent horse across a gorgeous terrain or find true love with a favored movie star. Despite their intense allure I classify these as dreams of fantasy, unfulfilled hopes, and vague desires—in other words, quite ordinary dreams.

Then there are the spectacular dreams—the ones that the dead use to come and visit and offer their messages of comfort and hope. These are the dreams I have had since I was a teenager.

Perhaps the dead choose to come in dreams because that is when our defenses are at their lowest ebb or do not exist at all. We are more vulnerable when we are deeply sleeping, and that creates a portal through which all manner of dream-time communications can occur. And I don't believe that one has to be a psychic or a medium to have these types of dreams—one just has to care and be open and have the heart that listens and the mind that accepts without judgment.

As a very young child the dead came to me in form, and after a lapse of time that equaled about twelve years they ceased coming in this manner and began to visit me in my dreams. I never questioned this switch on their part and simply accepted the wisdom of those who had died.

Dreamtime with the dead is an adventure and a joy. I am taken to fantastic places beyond this world that some call Heaven, and the vistas I find myself in are so beautiful and so peaceful and joyful that I would linger there forever. Many of the historical personages who visit me take me back to the past, and I am gracefully allowed admittance into their homes as they existed then.

And the messages the dead come to impart to me are as unforgettable as the landscapes presented.

Often, the messages from the dead are intense, and the person or pet utilizes this method to let me know that they are about to pass over or have recently died. This has happened to me on several occasions with humans and once with a pet. In fact, one of the most compelling ways of proving that a dream is actually a visit from a dying, recently deceased, or dead person or pet is the linkage to an actual death. This validation offers undeniable proof that the dream was not an ordinary one.

These dreams of validation are the ones I have.

Many of the dead who visit me in my dreams also come to impart advice or simply share time with me in a favored landscape of the past or present. I have had this occur many times over the years, and I feel deeply honored to have had this time with the dead—whether they be of family linkage, a friend, a pet, or a historical figure I revere.

I must repeat that the dreams of the dead I have had are totally unforgettable and vivid. Yet I also have a practical way of remembering them, and this is thanks to my grandfather, who gave me a spiral-bound red leather calendar notebook to write in when I was a young girl. This simple gesture started me on a lifetime of journaling, not only my daily events but also my magical and wonderful dream encounters with the dead.

It is a practice I continue to this day.

The Difference in Dreams

To me, ordinary dreams have a flat and *normal* feel. These dreams are more of the present, and even though they may have fantastical images, symbolic characters, or be inhabited by those who have died, the sensation is one of distantness and limited interaction. These ordinary dreams are the ones in which I find myself chasing elusive hopes and worries about daily current events across a mental landscape fraught over the years with job/financial/relationship concerns. Ordinary dreams are those that seem to be wiped away as soon as you awaken, and you find you often have difficulty remembering the precise details of the dream.

An example of this type of dream from my own personal experience is this: several months ago I voluntarily left a position I had held for a little over fifteen years because it no longer resonated with my particular soul's journey of wanting and needing to write full time. The years, the love, and the hopes I had poured into this job left an indelible mark on my psyche long after I dropped off the keys and resignation letter in my boss's mailbox. Understandably, the deeply ingrained routine I had kept for that length of time had made its mark on my subconscious mind, and the termination of that routine disrupted my life on every level. Enter the on-again/off-again dreams of the office, the people I had worked with, and the clients I had cared about and interacted with. In most of these dreams I was an observer and only occasionally a participant. There were no messages imparted to assist me with my days, and the sensation was more like watching a movie in which I had a bit part.

And while these everyday types of dreams may sometimes recur with a few evident changes of the players in the scenes, for me they lack the constantness and the golden-shine luster of the dreams wherein the dead come to visit with me.

The dream visits from the dead are so very different. There is a feeling of actually being in the presence of the departed—of seeing, smelling, and hearing the vistas they bring me to. These dreams are extremely powerful and have much more substance than the ordinary dreams because they sear themselves into my soul with their incredible *realness*. All the things that are lacking in an ordinary dream are present when the dead come to visit me in dreamtime. I am totally alert and aware and definitely do not feel like a bit player. The deep and abiding unconditional love that emanates from my dead loved ones is incredible. The sense of calm urgency of the messages both positive and negative they must impart to me resonates on a much higher level and transports me beyond the ken of mortal existence. I am no mere dreamer when I am with them, but truly abide with them in a dimension where we can communicate on equal terms.

Again, when the dead have come to communicate with me about their physical passing from the earthly plane and I later find that I have had the dream on the precise day or near the time of their death, I know beyond knowing that I have stepped out of the realm of the ordinary and into the realm of truth—a place of total reality. And because some of these dreams happened in tandem with an actual documented event—the death of my dream visitor—it is proof to me that I have been in the presence of the dead. These phenomenal just-dying dream visits from people I have known and loved will be recounted in later chapters about my first love, Butch; my dear friend, British actor Jeremy Brett; my half-brother; as well as my precious dog Mandy, who came to me in a dream just moments before her death to seek my permission to leave.

But whether the departed ones have been dead for many years or are just leaving earthly form behind, the sense for me is still the same. These people and animal visitors are real and tangible. The overwhelming desire of the human visitors is to give a message or to impart wisdom and comfort. The animal dream visitors nearly parallel the humans, but in a non-verbal manner. Both kinds of dream visitors are to be found in vistas that are both new and yet familiar to me.

There is nothing at all that is ordinary about a dream visit from the dead; in fact, it is an event quite extraordinary.

Remembering the Visits

Before the dead came to me in dreams they appeared to me in form. The first such occurrence was in 1954, when I was just three years old. After a life-altering experience at that age, my contact with the dead became almost an everyday event up until I was over halfway into my fifth year. From the age of five until my late teens there was a lapse when no visits occurred, and as I stated previously I have no real explanation for this.

I am able to remember each of those first-form visits with incredible clarity, which I attribute to several factors; the up-close and personal visits I had with the dead were unusual and beyond intense. Each one of these interactions seared itself into my youthful mind with such incredible vividness that I never doubted that I was in the presence of someone who was not at all like the humans I interacted with on a daily basis. For one thing, I could see through my spirit visitors. But my young self had no fear of these ghostly ones because I did not have the total adult comprehension of them as *dead*. I simply accepted them as people I could see through and nothing more. They didn't emit a fearsome aura, and the only thing I ever really noticed about some—not all—was that it was a slight bit colder the closer I got to them.

And then there is the unusual way that the dead communicate.

May We Talk?

Way back when I had my first interaction with the dead, I couldn't help but notice that they communicated quite differently than we do on Earth. Whether they came in form or dreams they usually spoke to me with what I called "mind-talk," or a sort of mental telepathy from their mind to mine. It is like listening to someone's voice that has bypassed your hearing and gone straight into your head. Communicating with the dead when I was a young child was relatively easy. In fact, it was both easy and fun, although I do remember that I initially covered my mouth with my hand so that I wouldn't speak to them in words but with mind-talk. But I caught on quickly, and after a few visits with the dead who came to me in form, I found that this way of communication felt quite natural.

Getting the Sensation

If I were to attempt to describe what it is like to visit with the dead in my dreams, I would liken it to having one foot firmly planted in the earthly realm and the other in their world. As long as the balance is maintained I am able for a short time to become a very privileged inhabitant of both places. Consequently, when I visit with the dead in my dreams, the sensation of actually being there totally unencumbered by any preconceived notions of the afterlife is incredible. The dreams are always random for me, and the dead always choose the landscape we will meet in as well as the duration of the dream visit—I am no medium who can summon spirits—and this goes for both departed humans and pets.

The sense is that these people and animals that have died are *real*. They are not see-through at all. They are as they were in life, and their personalities are not altered by death. The human dead wear the clothing they favored in life from the time period in which they lived. I must remark that I have yet to see a phantom either in earlier personal-form visits or dream visits dressed in long, flowing white gowns or funerary tuxedos. That is not to say they don't exist—it is just that the dead I communicate with are grounded in their own concept of reality.

Unlike the everyday dreams of the office or other mundane concerns, when the dead visit me in my dreams I retain all my personal attributes and I am fully present in their world. I can actually feel the warmth of the eternal sun on my body, smell the newly mown grass or blooming flowers, hear the calls of birdsong or the musical flow of a creek rushing over pebbles and stones. For the span of time I am with them I am fully involved in what they have to show or tell me. Being in their presence makes me feel more alive and vital than any everyday dream ever could—and therein, I believe, lies the vast difference between the two types of dreams, a difference that must be repeated.

One type of dream is ordinary and the other extraordinary.

Dead Time

The dead I have met in both form or dreams have no timetables and, as I know from experience, the concept of time as we understand it really doesn't matter to them any longer—something that makes perfect sense. In fact, I found that their time is totally different from ours. To them a dozen years or even a century seems like a few minutes. When I have been with them either in dreams or during a near-death experience, I find that time is suspended. Many of the dead who have come to me have been in spirit for many, many years, yet, to most of them, time has either stood still or reversed upon itself. Some still reside in the exact places they occupied on Earth and continue to pursue common everyday tasks, while others travel abroad to other dimensions or to earthly destinations and appear to find themselves totally at ease there. Many shun their death sites, while others cling desperately to that place or to their graves.

Most of the dead I have encountered either in form or in dreams have moved on after death to a realm of golden light, peace, and beauty. A great many of them inhabit homes and places that were familiar to them in life, and this is particularly true of historical figures that have come to me. And, in fact, my observation is that the earthly places that they return to or abide in bend to their creative will. They often dwell in a former home site that to them, and to me as a dream visitor, appears as it did when they were physically residing there. They do not see the place as inhabited by others, visited by thousands of tourists, demolished, or falling into a state of disrepair. To their eternal eyes all is as it was and ever shall be.

As for the length of a dream visitation, I can only linger in that gap between the worlds as long as the spirit being communicated with allows it. And I must state that it is always the spirit who calls a halt to the meeting—it has never been something that I have willed to start or end. The dead are in full control of the entire visit. When it is time for the meeting to be over, they are either summoned away or simply say they have to leave. I cannot plead with a spirit to stay with me in a dream, although I have many times wanted to do just that. I have to accept that their time with me is limited and let them go, thankful for their visit and hoping they will return as they are able.

Further, I have found that the actual time of day in my world is somewhat important.

Usually after falling asleep I have those ordinary chasing-the-rainbow dreams wherein I often find myself wandering through that old job site, a cathedral, or a school of some sort. Most of these dreams find me meandering through places where I am lost and somehow find my way out. Sometimes I recognize the people in these dreams; other times they remain in shadow or are an unusual blend of several personalities.

The time of day when the dead seem to be able to come to me easily is after three a.m. or if I happen to go back to sleep later in the morning after being up the night prior. Perhaps because I am more relaxed it makes it easier for the dead to come to me.

Of course, the dead who come with the messages of their own passing visit when the event is occurring or as soon afterward as possible. My beloved Jeremy came to me in the early morning hours. My half-brother came to me while I was taking an afternoon nap during the time he was dying. Mandy Dog also came to me during a nap I took while she was actually passing.

It is all quite amazing and very wonderful—and there are no limitations.

The Ouija Board and EVPs

There were two times in my life when I attempted to coerce the dead to visit me and give me a message, thus closing the gap between Earth and Heaven. The first attempt was in the fall of 1969 while I was in college and just after my dear grandmother had passed away.

Several of my college girlfriends and I decided to put our meager funds together and purchase a Ouija board. It was Halloween night, and we were very excited to use the thing. Of course, I was hoping to get a message from my grandmother.

We gathered in the dorm room of one of my friends and waited until nightfall. Several candles were lit and the five of us sat cross-legged on the floor with the board in the middle. There was some nervous giggling, and then we all placed a finger on the planchette and waited. Nothing happened. Then one of my friends asked a question: "When will I die?" The indicator under our fingers seemed to come alive, and it was as if it were a separate entity pulling us along to the answer it wanted to give. It spelled out the words MAYBE SOON.

We all pulled our fingers away in unison. Frightened, we quickly pushed the Ouija board and the indicator back in the box and put it away in the closet and didn't touch it again.

When the college year ended I was given custody of the game—which, I now knew, was not a game at all.

Back from summer vacation my friends and I got settled in our rooms and met up. But one of our members was missing. I found out that the friend who had gotten the MAYBE SOON message from the board had suffered a ruptured appendix shortly after leaving for summer break. She'd had emergency surgery and had almost died. The board had been close enough to being right, and that was terrifying to us.

As far as I know, none of us ever used the Ouija board again to contact the spirit world. After college ended in 1971 I still had the board with me, and it was stored in the attic of Pleasant View, the home my grandfather built and where I live today. One day in 1982, when the house was being renovated, I found the board and threw it into a bonfire on the property. I don't think I will ever forget the way that board died. It was thrown into a fire that was already burning down, but as soon as it hit the fire the flames shot up almost three feet into the air. And the sounds that came from it were terrible! It may have been the materials that the board was made of, but I don't think so, because the field echoed with shrieks and near-screams as the board was consumed by the flames.

I was very glad it was gone.

My second attempt at communicating with the dead on purpose was in 2009, when I attempted to do some EVP (electronic voice phenomena) work at Pleasant View with a digital recorder. It was a very cloudy and dreary summer day, and I set up the recorder in the kitchen. I noted the time and date on the tape and asked, "Is there anyone here who wishes to speak to me?" I left the room and sat at the dining room table, keeping myself very quiet. I repeated this question as I moved to every room in the house. When I played the recording back I had an amazing discovery. In no other room but the kitchen had I caught a voice. It was very deep and seemed very annoyed with me. It was definitely male and a voice I did not recognize, but in answer to my question it growled, "No!"

When one of my friends came to visit me shortly after the 2009 incident, we also attempted some EVP work but with no luck.

I have never tried again.

I have learned my lesson about attempting to contact the dead on my terms.

I will stick to the limited yet kindlier communications the dead offer me through my dreams.

How Do I Look?

Oddly enough, I often do not have the opportunity to look down and view my physical self when I am with the dead in dreams—that means to be able to see what clothes I am wearing, what footwear I have on, or if I am in my present body shape or have somehow regressed to a younger, svelter form (this last always being my personal favorite).

I believe it depends on how those who have passed on remember me as appearing. Some, like my first love, Butch, would always recall me as slim with short hair. So, when he has come to me in dreamtime that is usually how I appear. There are occasions in these dream visits when, for example, I have appeared as I do now and even my grandfather in particular doesn't seem to recognize me for the briefest of moments.

On the other hand, for those I have never met, such as historical personages, I apparently have the luxury of appearing in either my present form or as my slimmer and more youthful self.

This has always been a sort of puzzlement to me, but I have learned to accept it.

How the Dead Look

Most of the dead I have encountered in my dreams appear to have *youthened*—that is to say, that they grow younger—and some go all the way back to the way they looked as children. This process seems different for each individual. If they passed when they were forty or older, they appear to me to be about age thirty to thirty-five. This sometimes causes a bit of a problem with recognition, but that issue usually disperses within a few seconds of our meeting. There is always a quality of the spirit that remains familiar despite any alteration of the physical appearance. And sometimes the dead will change their appearance so that they are a blend of the old and the new, in order to be recognized more easily.

There are some who do not age backwards at all and appear as they were when they were nearing the end of their earthly lives. But even if they do not get younger, all of them seem so much happier, healthier, and vibrant. They glow with a great inner peace, and an awareness of eternity shines from their eyes. Even the departed pets I have met in either spirit form or dreamtime have gotten younger, friskier, and healthier. They run and jump about and seem full of the true happiness of no longer being encased in an ill or hurting body.

For all, both human and animal, there emanates from them the sense of the overwhelming joy they are experiencing of no longer being bound to the physical form.

May We Touch?

Another interesting fact I have found after being in the presence of the dead—whether they come in dreams or as their ghostly-form selves—is that they, for the most part and unless very special circumstances prevail, are not allowed to touch the living.

Because I am one of those people who enjoys hugging hello or goodbye, I am often cautioned or reprimanded by the dead when I make a move to embrace them. Just as the dead retain all of their earthly personality, I cannot change my impetuous self and so I usually attempt that hug. The dead always let me know when it is okay and when it is not.

Again, I do not question the wisdom of those who have passed, because they are still looking out for my own well-being.

That Dear Familiar Aroma

Everyone has a special scent that is associated with them during life. For some it may be a perfume or soap, or the smell of grease or oil, or anything and everything in between.

The aroma most associated with someone, the particular one that makes them known to the living, is the one that they carry with them to the afterlife.

One thing I noticed when the dead first began to come to me in form was that the aromas they brought with them identified them even if they did not appear in form or dreams. My grandfather's scent was always that of newly mown grass, cigarette smoke, and sweat, or even burnt autumn leaves. Grandma always smelled of talcum powder—specifically Cashmere Bouquet. Butch always announces his

presence with the scent of clothes freshly dried on the line
blended with spray starch, probably because he was so concerned with his appearance, and my dear friend British actor
Jeremy Brett heralds his visits to me with cigarette smoke
and a spicy and very haunting cologne scent that had emanated from one of the cards he sent me.

When the dead wish to let me know they are nearby but
not really willing or able to attempt a form or dream visit,
I find that their identifying scent drifts to my nostrils and I
know they have come to say hello or to check on me.

And this is always so very comforting.

Why No Visit?

One of the most puzzling things I have experienced with the
dead is the wonderment of why certain of them visit me in
dreamtime and others don't—or only stop by very briefly
and never return.

I was positive that my childhood friend, Sherry, who died
in the early 1970s in her twenties, would definitely come to
visit me after her death, but she never really did. The only
flutter of her presence was shortly after her funeral when
the heavy scent of roses wafted through a room where a
group of us were talking about her. Sherry and I had spent
most of our youth running through the fields and forests
that stretched for miles behind our homes. We had shared
our future dreams and many secrets, and created our own
imaginary worlds where we were always helping to rescue
others. For a time we were defined as "joined at the hip" and
couldn't really bear to be apart from one another for very
long. A few years after her death, I imagined that she somehow became a part of those hills and forests that we had

loved to race through, and that she roamed there once more eternally young and free and full of joy no matter what season of the year it was.

My father was another curiosity. He and I reunited at the home of a friend when I was sixteen, and that meeting was strained by the presence of other family and friends. Looking back, I now realize that even if I had been alone with him there would not have been any real attachment formed between us. At that point in my life I hadn't seen him since I was about two years old. I was also deeply involved in being in love with Butch and exploring the vast uncharted wonders of our new relationship. I was completing high school, applying to colleges, and mapping out my own destiny. By the time I re-met my father I had pretty much outgrown any real need for him in my life. But then, truth to tell and to be fair, my father and I did try several times in later years to build a tenuous connection, but it really was a waste of time because too much separation of our lives had occurred and too many regrets clouded any hopes we may have had of reconnection.

Then one day in the mid-1990s I heard from a friend that he was ill and that it was cancer. I did try to call the family, but I got nowhere and so I gave up.

I found out about his passing when I opened our local newspaper one July day and read his obituary and, saddest of all, noted that I had been omitted as a surviving child. This should not have been a surprise or bothered me, but it did—perhaps just because I had really tried to construct some sort of bridge between us where we might have at least shared a cup of coffee and some small talk alone at a local restaurant, but he never rose to the bait. He once told me that the half-hour drive from his home to mine was "too far."

I didn't shed a tear for him and I didn't attend his service. Perhaps that sounds unfeeling, but he had never really been a part of my life nor I of his, and I had to accept that. By the time I was a toddler he had already created a whole other life with a new wife and later other children and had distanced himself from me. Actually, I had no knowledge of his existence until I was almost nine and then only because I asked my grandpa if I had a "real" father after I was taunted by some of my classmates when I was in elementary school. Grandpa told me in no uncertain terms that he had no real liking for the man who had sired me, and that was based on his simple belief that no man had the right to abandon his child.

After I got the information from Grandpa, I remember I went outside to sit on my tree swing where I mentally digested the news. I soon came to my own conclusion about this unknown father and found his existence not relevant to my life. Grandpa told me that if I really wanted to meet my father he would think about arranging it, but he was against it. Knowing that my grandfather was wise beyond measure and trusting his judgment implicitly, I gave up wanting to bring about a meeting. To my mind my grandfather was my true father and the only one I would ever need in this world. When a friend's family suggested a meeting with my father, stepmother, and half-siblings when I was sixteen, I went more out of curiosity than anything else.

Still, after my father died I believed that our blood tie would be cause enough for him to pay me a visit, and so I waited for him to come to me after he passed and say something about our separation—but he never did.

All was silent.

In time, my hopes for my father to visit me in a dream became a distant echo, just as our earthly ties never really came to be.

I do wish him peace, and I hope that he is at last in that place where he is healthy and reunited with his loved ones.

There are many others whom I have known and loved and who passed without any fanfare, and again I either read their obituaries or heard by word of mouth that they had died. These were also people I spent a great deal of time with when I was growing up, yet they never came to me after their passing, although I expected them to.

One person who comes to mind was a high school friend named Jean. She died in the 1970s and didn't even cause a blip on my spiritual radar screen. She had moved to Ohio after high school, and we kept in touch via letters and phone calls while I was in college—and then all communication ceased. I thought nothing of it, being involved in healing from my grandparents' deaths, struggling with college classes, falling in and out of love, and then starting a new life and a new job. When I read her obituary and found out that the reason I hadn't heard from her was because she had been very ill and on life support at a hospital, I felt very badly about not keeping in touch with her.

A quiet, introspective girl, Jean slipped through the world and out of it as she had lived—not making a fuss about any of the details of living or dying.

Yet another interesting study was our dear neighbor, Dennis, who passed away in the early 2000s. He and my husband, Dan, had been very close, and when Dan found him dead on the floor of his living room, the shock waves of his passing burned through our hearts in bouts of crying and deep sadness. Dennis had been a big part of our lives for quite a few years. A British gentleman, he sought solace in our company and spent a great deal of time with us, especially around the holidays. We took him with us on drives out of town and had quiet evenings with him at Pleasant View and at his home, where we shared tea and cookies, great meals, and great conversations.

Dennis was a landscape artist who painted in oils, and he was extremely good at it. One of his beautiful paintings hangs in our home. When he began to develop health problems he gave up painting and seemed to fold in upon himself, slowly withdrawing from life and his creative side.

After he passed away I waited for a dream visitation from him, but the only hint of his interest in communicating with me came via a very quick dream of him boxing up his paintings and mind-talking with me about his lost hopes of being a publicly exhibited artist. He had spoken to Dan and me several times about trying to exhibit his artwork in local shops and galleries, but aside from one place he mentioned, he had never gone any further with it.

So, the very quick dream of him boxing up those paintings and supplies was a bit disappointing but very telling indeed.

It made me come to deeply consider the choices we make and the regrets and unfinished hopes we can carry with us into the next dimension. To me, this echoes back to Grandpa's wise advice to me when I was just entering my teenage years: "Leave this world a better place than you found it and leave with as few regrets as possible."

Dennis never returned to visit me and this, as well as his unfulfilled dreams of being an artist that mattered in the world, was very saddening.

Dennis and I did talk on a few occasions near the end of his life as he wondered what lay beyond. I did my best to reassure him.

In my heart I know that he has found the peace he so deeply craved and perhaps inspiration to paint in paradise.

Those Who Do Visit

It is often just as curious for me to ponder some of the spirits who do visit me in dreams—the ones I never really had a close relationship with or whom I have never met. These visitors include famous historical figures, an accident victim, and even a murdered man. Two of these, the accident victim and the murdered man, didn't really come to me in either dreams or form but more as shouts in my mind—but that is still a significant contact and one I don't take for granted.

The accident victim was a child who died after being hit by a vehicle. I recall that I was getting my breakfast ready, and a very young voice zinged through my head with something about a stuffed animal and "Tell Mommy." I had no idea why this voice would have come to me so urgently, and so I continued with my meal and cleanup. The next day I read the article in the newspaper about the death, and I thought back to that desperate little voice of the day prior and considered that must have been that child who had wanted my attention.

The murdered man was an off-duty state policeman who was shot during a robbery attempt. Driving past the spot where he was shot, a four-word sentence was shouted into my mind very quickly, "Tell Rose I'm okay!" I had never met the man in question and at first only told Dan about the odd visitation. Then one day I told one of my workmates at the office about the message I had received. She told me that Rose was the name of the dispatcher at the station house— something I wasn't aware of. Despite being urged to do so, I never delivered the message.

Neither the child nor the officer attempted communication again.

Dual Dreaming

My mother and I eventually reunited in my adult years. One day about ten years ago we experienced a very interesting dual-dream phenomenon that centered around the death of my half-brother in a propane explosion at his home.

This in-tandem dream visitation between my mother and me was truly remarkable.

It happened that I was napping that summer afternoon at my home, and my mother was also asleep at her home about an hour or so away from mine.

Suddenly I was dreaming and found myself standing by the side of a rutted and grass-covered dirt road that meandered through a summer forest and went off to my right into the sunshine. On either side of the road were meadows of tall yellow grass waving lazily in a warm breeze. Birds were singing in the distance and occasionally flitting past me and into the trees nearby. I could hear the sounds of small animals scuttling about in the dried leaves behind me. Other than the sounds of nature, all was silent as if the place I was in was holding its breath and waiting.

I looked up the road to my left and saw a male figure limping toward me. When he finally came even with me I saw that he was badly burned. He was tall and very thin and was wearing a T-shirt, jeans, and white sneakers. Half of his hair was burned away; his face was streaked with soot and blood; and his clothes and shoes were smoldering. He smelled of smoke and another underlying aroma that made me feel quite ill. I had to look at him several times before I recognized him as my half-brother.

He looked over at me sadly and then continued limping up the road toward the sunshine and a destination only he was aware of. He seemed to be in shock and did not mind-talk to me at all. The odd thing was that as he moved away from me he began to youthen from about age forty to about twelve. As he youthened, the apparel he was wearing seemed to change to a blue madras shirt, jeans, and new sneakers.

In the meantime, my mother was also dreaming of my half-brother. By her report, her dream was at the same location: on a country dirt road. The only differences were that in her dream my half-brother was running and that he mind-talked to her when she asked him where he was going. "To find my father," he replied. "You won't find your father on a dirt road," she said.

He then hurried off. My mother noted that he had the same appearance of being badly burned and that his clothes were the T-shirt-and-jeans combo that was smoldering. In her dream visitation with him, he was barefoot and he did not youthen. As he ran off in search of his father, his outfit did not change.

Neither one of us had any idea that he had died within moments of those dreams in an explosion at his home. However, when my mother was told of his death and she called me, we shared our grief and then told one another of the dreams we'd had that afternoon. We discovered the dream visits were very near the time of my half-brother's actual death.

It was apparent to both of us that not only did we share an incredible connection, but also that her son and my half-brother had wanted very badly for both of us to know that he had died.

I am often asked by a friend or family member why it is that the spirits of those they have loved and who have passed on come to me and not to them. For this question I have no real answers.

My experiences with the dead have led me to believe that they seem to *know* who will be receptive to them and who will not. Perhaps they don't appear to the ones they've left behind because they believe the pain of seeing them again would be too hurtful, and so they find a sympathetic person with an open mind and do their best to communicate.

Perhaps they are also afraid that if they come to a loved one in a dream or form they will be brushed off as a mere hallucination or a nightmare.

And that would be very sad.

A Few Revelations

A great many of the experiences I have had are very contrary to what I was taught via my Catholic upbringing. Back in the days of my youth when I attended religious instruction in my grandfather's chosen faith, I came to learn that Heaven was a reward granted to selected people who had "done good deeds" and thus were allowed to enter the Kingdom of Heaven with their pure hearts and souls intact. While many were allowed admittance to Heaven, only those with the purest of hearts eventually became saints. Unbaptised infants went to a realm somewhere between Heaven and Hell called Limbo. If one died in adulthood but had a few venial sins dotting their soul, well then, they went to a place called Purgatory and waited there for prayers and intercessions to release them to Heaven. Once attaining Heaven, the soul was met by St. Peter at a golden gate and an assessment of the just-left earthly life was begun. If the soul passed all the requirements presented, they were admitted to that oh-so-coveted kingdom.

Of course, those who had been extremely "bad" during life ended up in Hell, where Satan kept his eternal barbecue pit going full blast and one was tortured for all time for their sins by those hot flames.

But my dream visits with the dead and near-death experiences have taught me otherwise.

The afterlife I have wandered through in my dreams and near-death experiences has no boundaries of religious belief. All are one. All are united.

During two of my three near-death experiences I have been met by my guardian angel, and access to Heaven within the protection and guidance of this being of light was swift. Once there, the all-encompassing sensation is like being immersed in the most beautiful and indescribable sense of total peace and love that knows no boundaries. There is no judgment in Heaven. There is only acceptance and total joy and a soul sense of finally being *home* at last.

Another interesting revelation for me was to find that there are different levels of ascension on the other side. New arrivals are at what I would deem Level One. They are usually the most confused and act like students on the first day of school in a new building. There is sometimes panic, but not always. Often the spirit guide who was to have come for the new arrival hasn't made an appearance at the precise moment of death for the initiate so they wait either patiently or impatiently (when we meet "Gramma" Irene in a later chapter, this will be a bit clearer).

After the meeting-and-greeting portion of the transition is complete, the spirit seems to almost immediately learn a new way to communicate utilizing mental telepathy. They use this to "speak" to one another and to the living. This new skill, as I noted, is not at all difficult to learn and, like any new achievement once it is learned, it is not forgotten. Of course, there are some who initially still wish to communicate with me in the regular Earth way with their voice, but they eventually do learn to mind-talk.

Level Two seems to involve the spirit letting go and being let go of by those still on the earth plane. Many times those who have come to me in spirit will speak about how a loved one's crying or grieving cut through them "like a knife" or "hurt" deeply. From this I have gathered two things: first, that the dead feel our sadness acutely; and second, that they cannot progress forward on the path of their new life because the intense emotions of those left behind keep them stuck on the earth plane.

I feel in my heart that this is exactly what happened with my dear grandfather. Despite the fact that I knew as a young child that the soul survives and that the person who loved me is as nearby me as possible in spirit, as an eighteen-year-old girl losing both of the people who had been my only parents left me abandoned and very lost. I adored both my grandparents, but it was especially difficult for me to come to terms with the physical absence of my grandfather. His dying gouged the most incredible deep hole in my psyche, and so I mourned his passing intensely and for many years after the actual event. Actually it wasn't until almost fifteen years after Grandpa's death that I finally let go of him, and as you will read in the chapter about him, my grieving, as I said, may have delayed his progression to the next level.

Truly then and despite any limitations I may undergo with the dead, I have found that there is only simplicity and love and a unique fairness to what most of them experience—they appear to gain some skills when they let go of physical form, but they don't become all-knowing or omnipotent.

Grandma McNally with her son, Edward Junior, in about 1927

Oddly, sometimes their knowledge of their circumstances is either very expansive or quite limited, and this, I believe, is due to the shock of finding themselves in non-physical form—or of never really coming to terms with being dead.

"Hello! My Name Is Edward."

One particular spirit I met in form when I was four years old was very forthcoming with some information about the process of dying and his perceptions of Heaven and the afterlife. This was my grandparents' son, Edward Junior, who died at age nine. He appeared to me in form only. When I first met him in the upstairs of my home he introduced himself by saying simply and with mind-talk, "Hello! My name is Edward." After we had gotten to know one another I asked him what Heaven was like, and I remember he said it was "nice." I was, at that time, very curious about angels and asked him if he had seen any. His response was somewhat revealing but also joyfully nonchalant: "Oh, yes! There are many who glow with a beautiful light around them. They move quickly. They are always rushing. They are very nice."

Edward and I were operating on a virtually unbalanced yet level playing field due to age and experience. At the time I was asking him these questions I was about four and he was eternally nine. He had lived and died and had found a way back to the earthly plane. I was of the earth, and yet by that time I had a pretty secure foot in his realm as well. So, to me, his mind-talk answers to my questions were easily understood.

I asked him once, "Were you afraid to die? Did it hurt?"

He was thoughtful and then said: "It wasn't scary and it didn't hurt. The angels came for me. I could see them from my bed, and I just drifted over to them and we left."

He paused. "But I didn't like to see my mother crying when I had to go. That hurt awful bad."

So, Edward was a companion in spirit for about two years who gave me one of my first pieces of proof that the dead are ever with us, that they are able to transfer themselves between the dimensions at will, and that our grieving for them can keep them earthbound.

The In-Between Place

I have only encountered one spirit, that of my father-in-law, who was both perplexed and relieved at finding himself in a "gray" area shortly after his sudden death from a heart attack. He called it alternately both a "holding place" and a "resting place," and it seemed as though, to me at least, that he was comfortable there in that in-between place—neither moving forward nor backward in his spiritual journey until he was ready.

One Nasty Old Woman

Just as there are the wonderful and joyous visits from the dead who are imbued with such positivity and radiance, I must state that I have also had one dream visit from a very negative spirit. This happened about ten years ago and was over very quickly, probably because within the dream I stood my ground with her. I truly believe that the strength I found during my first near-death experience at age four helped me through this. This was a spirit that would be termed a hag. She appeared seated in a very dark room. She was hideous to look upon and had long, scraggly hair and razor-sharp fingernails. She seemed to want my soul, and her power was deeply felt. I drew away from her and mentally told her "No!" and she faded away, never to be seen again. I do not know why she came to me or what her story was. Suffice it to say that I was very glad to see her leave, and I hope never to meet her again.

I had an indication of the realm that such as this hag would occupy when, during one of my three near-death experiences, I was given a sort of divine knowing that beyond the beautiful vista to which I was allowed admittance was another place where there was no light, no joy, and very little hope. Still, I didn't get the impression that it was the commonly held interpretation of Hell that I grew up with—a place of eternal fire and brimstone and demons running about and torturing the unfortunates—but I sensed that this was a very, very dark place where the souls imprisoned there had many lessons yet to learn before they would even be considered for release.

A Comforting Experience

I cannot even begin to express here how much comfort, courage, and hope I have received over the years from all my visits with the dead—from personal visits, dream visits, mind-shouts, and from my own three near-death experiences. There is such great reassurance offered during each one of the encounters.

How marvelous and what a privilege it has been for me to be able to meet caring people from history who welcome me into their times, to see once more my beloved pets scampering and rushing about totally healthy and enjoying themselves, and then to actually spend time with my loved ones who have passed—to see them vibrant and full of an eternal peace and a great *knowing*. They do not feel the pain of whatever illness or accident or event took them away from

Pleasant View Service Station, circa 1930. In the foreground
are Grandpa McNally and son Edward Junior.
Grandma McNally is at the window.

earthly life. They are full of joy and have a continued great
interest in us and our ongoing lives here on Earth—although
they cannot interfere, they are able to offer advice and convey
concern if we have hearts and minds that are open and willing to listen.

And when our time here is done, all those we have loved
and who have loved us will be waiting with open arms, ready
to hold us close and welcome us *home*.

chapter two

My Journey Begins

My Early Years

I came to live with my grandparents when I was a newborn and was to stay with them until they passed away when I was eighteen. But long before I arrived in their lives they had known unendurable sadness and tragic loss. All three of their dear children had died at very young ages, leaving my grandparents grief-stricken on a level I cannot even imagine. My grandfather once told me that my grandmother had been "inconsolable," and he had feared that he would lose her as well. Because of this, they drove to an orphanage in Albany, New York, and chose a blonde-haired, green-eyed toddler girl from the hundreds of children there because, according to Grandpa, she "looked so much like our own." A few years later they finalized the adoption of my mother.

My mother and father were married after high school, and about a year later I was born.

By the time I was taking my first breath it was reported that my father had pretty much abandoned both my mother and me. My grandfather came to the rescue and offered a solution to the situation that would benefit all concerned—my grandparents would take care of me while my mother went off to pursue her education as a nurse.

Thus it was that I came to live at Pleasant View, the home my grandfather had built in the early 1920s. Here on the outskirts of the rural community of Oneonta, New York, he would open a service station/restaurant and enjoy many profitable years in that venture until he closed the business in the early 1950s.

These dear people doted on me when I arrived in their lives, and I knew at a very young age that I was cherished beyond measure. I eventually learned that their oldest son, the aforementioned Edward Junior, had been struck by a car in front of the house during the winter of his ninth year and died shortly afterward in a local hospital. Junior's two sisters, Gene Ann and Cathleen Dora, had both died as toddlers—one from peritonitis and one from pneumonia.

So it was that death and mourning and tragedy had already settled oh-so-deeply into the fiber of Pleasant View, imbuing it with a sense of timeless sadness.

From my earliest recollection I seemed to resonate to something unseen but tangible within the house. Indeed, the structure always seemed to me to be a living thing that had about it a yearning that was incredibly real. And as I was always extremely sensitive to such things from the time of my infancy, the house became a part of the structure of my being and I of it. I sensed that we were somehow joined on a cosmic level and that we resonated deeply to one another. As I grew to adulthood I became a part of the soul being of the place, and its sorrows and joys entwined in my psyche. To this day I still reside at Pleasant View with my husband, Dan, and our sweet cat, Pretty, and the house still exudes that restless desire to cleanse its sad history.

My early days at Pleasant View were remarkable for finding joy in every moment. A solitary child, I meandered through a world of beauty and peace. My toddler days were marked by holding onto Grandma's dress or Grandpa's calloused and gentle hand and roaming through flower beds of sweet scented peonies, roses of every hue, hollyhocks, gladiolus, daisies, and so much more—and by the time I was three I knew the names of every one of the flowers that graced the property. In the springtime of my youthful days there were newly hatched baby chicks to care for and a large garden to plant and tend.

Life was full of contentment, peace, and love.

Then came the bout with pneumonia, the first neardeath experience, and the opening of the portal that allowed me to communicate with the other side.

Grandpa's Wisdom

As I previously mentioned I am grateful to my grandfather for many things, but most especially for my openness to communication with the dead. He was the one who regaled me with tales of ghosts, leprechauns, and pixie folk that he had seen when he was growing up in his native Ireland. Apparently, there was no shortage of these phenomena in his homeland. It also seemed to me that Grandpa had carefully memorized every single otherworldly tale and experience from his younger days so that he could one day share them with an appreciative audience.

When I was about age three, he deemed me ready to be that audience.

How well I remember sitting on Grandpa's lap by the big black kitchen woodstove during crispy-cool autumn evenings as the chill breezes pressed against our little home. With Grandma seated nearby and combing out her long gray hair before bedtime and the Baby Ben alarm clock ticking off the minutes on the counter, I snuggled my head against Grandpa's shoulder and settled in. The wood in the grate snapped and crackled, and the delightful warmth invited drowsiness. I clutched my brown and gold teddy bear and my blue and yellow baby blanket and relaxed into the sound of Grandpa's heartbeat against my cheek and his deep mesmerizing voice.

Grandpa always cleared his throat a couple of times before beginning any story—just for the effect, and this always made me giggle quietly. He also began every tale with "Once upon a time," speaking in his matter-of-fact way about those long-ago days of his boyhood in that mystical and magical place known as Ireland. Sometimes the story would be about a leprechaun he and his brothers had chased as they tried to catch the little fellow and make him give up his pot of gold. Other stories were about seeing wee fairy folk dancing on sunbeams or flower petals.

But my very favorite stories were the ghostly ones. He spoke of passing by a churchyard near his home during the still-dark early morning hours and seeing the wispy figures of the dead drifting about the headstones. Apparently these spirits always seemed to moan and wail a lot, and Grandpa always mimicked their sounds for me. Grandpa said these spirits were "lost" and "lonely" or "bound to the earth," and that they were not at all interested in harming the living— although he did admit that he tended to "walk a bit faster" past the graves if it were a particularly dark night devoid of moonlight.

While in Ireland, Grandpa had been employed for a time as a gravedigger. He told many gooseflesh-raising tales of how he often had to dig up an old grave and place a new coffin atop the one already residing there. Often the coffin of the previous resident had rotted through, and Grandpa could clearly see the remains of the last dearly departed. "Nothing at all to be scared of, Johnny," he would tell me, using his tomboy nickname for me. "The only things left were some bones, teeth, and bits of rotted clothing. The soul had usually flown away long ago."

From the time my grandfather had been a youth to the time he was sharing his stories with me and up until his own death, he had never shown any fear of dying. This may have been partially due to the fact that the wakes he was a part of in Ireland were more celebratory than mournful. He saw them as a co-mingled time of both sadness and celebration of the soul's release from the body and being free at last.

Later, as a custodian at a local hospital, Grandpa had a hair-raising experience that he just loved to share with me over and over. One night, as was sometimes his duty, he had to take a corpse to the morgue that was located in the basement of the facility. When he told the story of how one of those corpses "sat straight up on the gurney" after he had put it in the morgue, I shrieked with shivery fear. Grandpa remarked, "That dang-near scared me to death!" I simply loved this goosebump-raising tale.

So it is that I attribute my lack of anxiety about death at such a young age to Grandpa's stories and nonchalant attitude about death and dying. Grandpa's theory about the subject: "Nothing to be afraid of. It's just a going to sleep in one place and waking up in another."

Grandpa's easy way of communicating his wisdom came during our many hikes into the fields and forests behind Pleasant View, where we often went on a summer evening or to go berrying.

These kinder and sweeter lessons were usually given at the end of our hike or berrying time. We often paused beneath the shade of a stately oak tree that guarded the pathway home. We would sit down side by side and converse on whatever topic was on our minds. I well recall one particular late August day in the summer of my ninth year when he gave me such a lesson I shall never forget and one that points to his understanding of the cycle of life, death, and renewal.

Grandpa had been seated on the ground beside me and we had been sitting quietly, just listening to the sounds of crickets waking up and birds chirping as they got ready for bed. We were enjoying the coming of near-twilight when Grandpa suddenly stood up and put his hands on the trunk of the old oak. I stood up with him. "See this old oak tree? It's been around probably longer than I've been alive, but it's still here. It has gotten through storms and terrible cold winters. It dies every year and comes back to life again in the spring. It has sap for blood, and it feels pain and sadness like we do. And, when it is time for it to die, it will know."

He bent down and picked up some acorns and held them out to me. "And these acorns are its children, and if one or more of them are lucky enough they won't get eaten by squirrels or chipmunks but will get into the dirt and grow into oak trees just like this one."

I looked up at the sturdy branches of the tree with its broad, green leaves rustling gently in the warm and nearly nighttime breeze and felt a sudden kinship to it. Knowing that it was a real living thing that could *feel* brought a deeper clarity to my life. After that night I saw the tree and all plants as entities that had the ability to deal with all sorts of things and yet survive and return again and again until they, like the pets I had loved and lost, would die and perhaps be reborn through their children.

This was a revelation that stuck with me and eventually ushered into my mind the larger picture of my own life as I hurtled toward adulthood.

Grandpa's wisdom was impeccable, and his lessons were always given with such clarity and simplicity that they easily sank deeply into my own soul. Grandpa always seemed to me to be larger than life and to have incredible knowledge of everything. He taught with lessons that were easily under-stood and fair, and, best of all, he never seemed to preach or to create any boundaries in my life other than those of kind-ness and morality and always treating others exactly the way I would want to be treated. His kindness and compassion ex-tended to every living thing—not just people, but to all of the earth and nature's creations, and that included trees as well as animals, and even, much to my dismay, the residents of the insect world—except, of course, the hornets or yellow jackets that dared to build their nests near Pleasant View.

My First Near-Death Experience

During the winter of 1954 I was three years old and dying of pneumonia.

My grandparents had summoned a doctor to the house, and on his advice I had been taken to the local hospital and admitted.

Because I was so weak and ill I had no real concept of time passing, until I awoke groggily to find myself in a corridor bed with a clear plastic tent around it. This of course was the oxygen tent that was helping me to breathe. I looked out through slitted eyes at a world that was strange and blurry and very scary and lonely. All the distant sounds of metal carts rattling by and voices were muted and seemed to be coming from a very great distance. The smell of antiseptic was overpowering. All these things combined intensified my feelings of fear and isolation.

Imagine my astonishment when I heard a young girl's voice calling my name very clearly and urgently. "Marilou! Marilou! Get up! It's me, Emmie!" I could barely open my eyes at all, but when I did I saw before me the face of a very pretty girl of about six or so. She was dressed in a pale blue silky dress with a high lace collar. She had bouncy blonde curls and twinkly blue eyes. Her smile was brilliant, and her perky personality made me feel even worse.

I just wanted to go back to sleep—to drift into the darkness and not feel the pain any longer.

"Marilou! Come play with me! You'll like it here! I know you will!"

Even in my very ill state I realized that Emmie wasn't talking to me the way I knew how to talk with my mouth. She was communicating to me in my head. I never saw her lips move or her mouth open or close, but her shrill and very demanding voice echoed in my mind. Then the vista suddenly changed before me, and I felt myself somehow drift into a sunlit meadow with Emmie and heard the screeches of joy from hundreds of other children. Not one mouth moved, but the meadow was full of the sound of laughter and fun-filled shouts. So many children were there of all colors and sizes, all playing tag or chase or "Ring Around the Rosie"— all happy. They appeared to be between the ages of three to six or a bit older.

Emmie held out her hand to me, and I remember backing away and putting my hands behind my back. I sensed on some level that it would be a very bad thing to take her hand and stay with her and those children in that sunlit meadow.

I don't know how it happened, but Emmie, the children, and the meadow suddenly faded away and I found myself once more on the bed. It took a lot of my strength, but I recall pushing my hands under my back so that Emmie couldn't get them in hers if she returned.

I was so very tired and just wanted to let the sleepiness drag me down.

I was about to close my eyes when a very bright light began forming outside the tent. Oddly, the brilliance didn't hurt my eyes at all. As I watched, the light formed itself into a sort of oblong shape and drifted up into the corner of the hallway ceiling where it hovered, emitting a feeling of perfect love and peace and protection. I watched it until I fell asleep in the comfort of its presence.

Emmie did return on several other occasions, and each time she did the light would move down from the ceiling and stay outside my bed until she left.

One day I woke up, opened my eyes, and looked around. I was still feeling weak but a bit stronger. Then I noticed that the light was outside my tent and seemed to be in a glowing human form. It spoke in my mind: "Wake up now, Marilou. You are healed."

I remember struggling to pull myself to a sitting position. I was very hungry and thirsty and extremely shaky, but I managed to find the strength to begin hitting against the plastic cover. A nurse came and looked in at me and left. She came back with the same doctor who had come to see me at my home. A few hours later I was in a room with another child.

In my later years, Grandpa told me that I had stayed in the hospital for an additional two weeks before I came home.

When I returned to the sweet embrace of my beloved Pleasant View and my grandparents' love, I pondered for a short time on what had happened to me at the hospital.

I had no way of knowing that several momentous things had happened to me: I'd had my first near-death experience, visited paradise, met my guardian angel, and been healed of a deadly disease.

My First Funeral

It was 1955 and the spring of my fourth year. My grandparents decided to take me to my first funeral at our local Catholic church. I recall that we were all dressed in our Sunday-best clothes and that while getting ready there seemed to be a great solemnity hovering over the day. I also thought it odd that we were going to church on a day that was not a Sunday, but I kept the feelings and thoughts to myself, preferring to let the day unfold and to enjoy whatever adventure it might bring.

Little did I know that an adventure of a sort I never anticipated was waiting for me.

At the church we sat in a pew near the back, which was unusual, as we usually sat about ten rows back from the altar in the center aisle. There was nothing to be done about it so I relaxed, enjoyed the different view, and stayed quiet. I sat primly between my grandparents, my white-gloved hands folded on my lap, and I spent a lot of time admiring my shiny black patent leather shoes and my lacy white socks.

When the organ music began we all stood. There was a commotion to my left in the lobby. A few minutes later a large, shiny wooden box with part of the lid open was wheeled up the aisle. The priest and altar boys came down to the box. The priest began saying a prayer, and one of the boys was swinging what looked like a small metallic lantern on a chain. Soon afterward the church began to smell of an acrid odor that burned my nostrils—this, I later learned, was incense and was part of the funeral rites.

Just before we sat down I saw a movement near the box. A very nice-looking older lady wearing a dark-colored dress was standing there. I could see right through her to the altar beyond. She looked very sad and kept reaching out to a group of people seated on the front row of pews to her right. They didn't pay any attention to her, and I thought it odd that they couldn't see her. She was standing right next to them. She looked like she was going to cry and then seemed to recover and looked right at me. She waved hello very carefully. Now seated, I glanced at my grandparents. Grandma was praying her rosary and Grandpa's eyes were shut as he too prayed. I quickly risked a cupped hand wave to the lady. She smiled at me, looked forlornly at the people in the front pew again, and vanished.

After the mass was over, the box was wheeled to the back of the church and into the lobby. Ushers allowed the few scattered mourners out row by row, and these people all filed past the box quietly and made the sign of the cross on themselves. Most looked stony-faced after they peered into the box. Some were crying softly and blowing their noses.

When it was our turn, Grandpa picked me up and carried me to the box.

I looked down.

There lying very, very still was the lady who had waved to me at the beginning of the mass.

Grandpa whispered to me, "This woman in the coffin was a great friend to your grandmother and me. She just died a few days ago. Give her a kiss goodbye."

As Grandpa lowered me down, I gripped the side of the box. The closer I got to the body of the woman in the blue dress, the more I felt that *nothing* was there except a vast emptiness and a weary solitude.

I recalled all those stories Grandpa had told me about dead people in coffins and looked a bit closer. I was thankful I didn't see "bones and teeth" in the box.

I leaned over and kissed the woman's cheek. It was hard and cold and not at all like the talcum powder–smooth face of my grandmother.

On the way home I sat in the back seat of the car and pondered what had just happened, but there were no easy answers.

I now recognized death as a vast emptiness, yet despite the coldness emanating from the body in the coffin, the lady had appeared to me and seemed quite well even though very sad.

In my mind I was beginning to put quite a few things to-gether—death was not really the end, as had been shown to me during my hospital stay and at the funeral. The body was stored away in the coffin, much like clothing I had outgrown was stored in the old steamer trunk upstairs or given away because it was no longer of any use.

Clarity was coming to me.

The funeral had made me very tired, and I put my head back against the seat and drifted off to sleep.

I would keep the old woman's visit a secret for many years to come, just as I would the experience with Emmie and the beautiful being of light. I eventually told Grandpa shortly before he died, and afterward he shared with me a near-death experience dream of Heaven he'd had shortly after one of his heart attacks.

My First Cemetery Visit

After the funeral of the woman, my communication with the dead kicked into overdrive. It was as if the departed ones had been waiting and were now clamoring for my attention. Several things happened simultaneously.

The most amazing was the aforementioned meeting in spirit with the ghost of my grandparents' lost son, Edward Junior, who appeared to me in the upstairs of Pleasant View, and, as noted, spent about two years with me, playing and mind-talking about his own death, his lost sisters, and Heaven, and playing silly mental word games.

The second was a ghostly interaction that occurred during my first visit to the cemetery where Edward Junior and my grandparents' two little daughters, Cathleen Dora and Gene Ann, were buried. (Grandpa always referred to them as "the wee angels.") Also in the cemetery was a tombstone honoring my grandfather's brother, John, who had died during World War I.

Because this was the first time I had been taken to the cemetery, the indelible memories of that day are etched forever in my mind down to the slightest details. As a child gifted with incredibly vivid recall, this day stands out as a hallmark one in my life.

It was Memorial Day of my fourth year. We had gone to a local greenhouse about a week before and bought a great many red, white, and pink geranium plants. Grandpa had confided to me that while most of them were for the flower beds at home, four of them were for "the graves."

On the day we were to go to these graves, Grandma prepared a picnic lunch and packed it in the old wooden basket.

She also made up a thermos of hot coffee and a mason jar of iced tea. Grandma and I got dressed in our Sunday-best clothes and I had to wear my Easter bonnet with the elastic that hurt my neck. Grandpa sported tan slacks, a second-best nice plaid shirt, and a brown button-up sweater with a V-neck.

The plants, some digging tools, and a jug of water were put in the trunk of the car as well as the picnic basket and a blanket, and we were off.

I had no idea where we were going and so settled in for a long journey. I hoped we were headed to the county fair or maybe to Otsego Lake in Cooperstown, New York, both spots about a half-hour from our home and two of my especial favorites.

It was only a few minutes after we left the driveway that Grandpa had the turn signal on and we were driving through a black wrought-iron gate onto a roadway that went uphill. I sat up and looked out the window, but all I could see were rows and rows of white stones. Grandpa turned left and parked in front of a sort of garage, got out, and began to unload the trunk. He spread the blanket under the shade of a nearby big maple and put the picnic basket there.

Grandma got out and opened my door, and I hopped out and looked around.

The day was warm and breezy. Over our heads blue jays flew past, screeching their eternal "Thief! Thief!" Some squirrels ran up and down the maple, scolding us for disturbing their afternoon romp.

Grandma took my wrist in her hand, and while Grandpa carried the geraniums and jug of water, we crossed the road and went up a bank. I tried to walk beside Grandma but she pulled me behind her, keeping us close to the back of the stones as we followed Grandpa. Grandma stopped and pointed to the stones on my left. "Do you see those, child? Those are graves. We don't step on graves. We show respect to the dead. Now, say you're sorry."

I didn't see anything or anyone to say sorry to but a stone with a photo of a young man in uniform on the front of it. "Sorry." I said, quietly. Immediately a man's voice echoed in my head, "It's okay, kid."

That was at least familiar, and I was happy that someone had responded.

Just ahead of us Grandpa had come to a stop by a large gray granite stone with writing on it. Grandma let go of my hand, admonishing me to stay close. While they went to the rear of the large stone and knelt down by two smaller stones, I went around to the front of the large monument and put my index finger in the letters, tracing them carefully. I knew the first and second letters were *M* and *C*.

Grandpa came over to me for a minute and patted the big stone. "This is where your grandmother and I will be buried when we die," he said quite matter-of-factly. I looked up at him, his gray-blue eyes smiling down at me, and felt no fear. I knew that even if he and Grandma did die one day that they would never leave me. Grandpa had already explained to me that when they died only their bodies would be gone. Their spirits would always be able to watch over me.

Grandpa returned to Grandma's side. I lingered for a few minutes looking down the hillside at the many stones with names on them and longed to go explore, but I stayed put, tracing the letters over and over again with my index finger.

Getting bored I went around to watch my grandparents, who were busy clearing away grass by the little stones, digging holes, and pushing the potted geraniums into them. Grandma was crying softly. I went over and knelt down beside her and rubbed her arm gently. "Grandma, are you all right?"

Grandpa stopped digging and took my hand. "Leave her be, Johnny," he said, using his tomboy nickname for me. "She's sad because this is where Junior and the two wee angels are buried."

I looked down.

Grandpa pointed to the stone in front of him. "This is where Junior is buried. Over there by your grandmother is where the two little girl angels are buried."

I got up and sat down next to Grandpa and put my hand on the grass over Junior's grave, rubbing it gently, trying to send soothing thoughts through the ground to my ghost friend even though I didn't really believe he was in there.

"Junior is really in here?" I asked, still patting the grass in front of the stone.

"Yes." Grandpa said, his voice heavy with unshed tears. "His soul has gone to Heaven—only his body is here. That's what happens when you die. You know that. Your body is put into a coffin or box, and that is put in the ground and your family places a stone with your name on it on top of your grave so you can be found and people can bring flowers and spend time with you."

I got up on my knees and looked at him. I was gaining more and more knowledge about death, yet just as many other details about the subject were confusing.

I longed to talk to Grandpa about everything I was wondering, but I kept my silent counsel, knowing that this was not the right time to bring up such a topic.

When we finished with the children's graves we went back across the road and put flowers in front of John's stone, and then we all sat down on the blanket to eat our picnic lunch of ham on wheat bread, homemade oatmeal-raisin cookies, and iced tea for Grandma and me with coffee for Grandpa.

Afterward, Grandpa took a picture of Grandma and me (the photo Grandpa took is in the frame on the cover of this book), and then, while Grandma and I relaxed, he went over by the car to smoke and, as he always said, "to cogitate," or have some deep thoughts. I could only imagine what things flitted through his mind as he stood there a short distance away from us—his face in the shade of the maple, his eyes looking over toward the graves of his lost son and daughters.

I looked up at my grandmother. She was sitting on the blanket next to me with her hands folded in her lap and appeared to be almost dozing. I knew she wasn't. She was in that in-between state of acceptance and crying and doing neither at that moment. She did not look across the road at the spot where her dear children were buried. She did not look at Grandpa or me. Both of my grandparents seemed wrapped in their own invisible places of isolation—united in sorrow and longing for a time that would never be again.

I moved closer to Grandma, and she put her arm around me and drew me close to her. I put both my arms around her and held her, hoping to somehow dispel the gloom of this place that was drenched in both sunshine and sadness.

She leaned against me and seemed to draw strength from my presence.

My mind turned over and over as I nestled against Grandma and watched Grandpa cogitate. He hadn't moved. He stood leaning against the car and smoking his cigarette. The wind blew gently down the hill, carrying with it the scents of spring and renewal. The birds flitted about the limbs of the tree above his head. Robins hop-skipped across the grass, and the squirrels were back and chasing one another up and down the trunk of the maple.

I saw that in the midst of the death the cemetery represented that life still flowed. Animals and birds still came to the cemetery. We were here to visit. And a couple of other cars came up the drive and parked far off in another section where Grandpa had told me the babies were buried.

I sat up and looked around. I was a little bored and thought perhaps I'd like to explore this place and see if there might be any other friendly voices like the one that had spoken to me after I mistakenly stepped on his grave.

I asked Grandma if I could get up and walk around a little.

Grandma said it was okay but to stay in sight.

I wandered along the rows of stones, making certain not to step on any more dead people.

A short space away from where my grandma sat on the blanket, I found a fascinating stone with a photo of a little girl about my age on it.

She looked very friendly.

Suddenly I heard a girl's voice in my head say, "Hello! Who are you?"

I looked and there was the girl in the photo standing next to the stone. One of her hands rested atop it as if it were a link of some sort or as if she were claiming it as her own. I could see right through her to the lawn and stones behind. She also appeared to me to be somewhat out of focus as if she were underwater or behind a ragged lacy curtain.

She shielded her eyes and mind-talked to me.

"I'm Beverly. Are those your parents?" She pointed at my grandparents.

"No, those are my Grandma and Grandpa. I'm Marilou." I hesitated. "Are you dead?"

She smiled the same sad smile as the old lady at the church had. "I'm sure of it."

"Did you get hit by a car like Junior?"

"No. I don't think so. I didn't mind my parents and something bad happened to me. I only remember floating and then I was someplace else and couldn't find my way home."

"Oh," I said. "That sounds sad."

"It is. My parents were here and they were crying. I miss them. I wish they would come back to visit me."

"Is your body in the ground by that stone?" I asked, pointing to the monument with her picture on it.

"I guess so," she said quietly in my mind.

"Can you come play or do you have to stay here?" I mentally asked.

"I have to stay here all the time. I'm waiting for my parents to come back to me. If I leave I might miss them."

"Why can't you just play for a minute? If they come we'll be right here."

"No. I'll stay here. I feel safe by this stone."

Before I could respond, Grandma called me to come on over so we could get ready to leave.

I looked at Grandma and then turned around to say goodbye to Beverly, but she had vanished. Used to the abrupt leave-takings of my see-through friends, I wasn't concerned.

On the way home my grandmother said, "I think the dead enjoyed our visit today. Don't you think so, Edward?" And Grandpa responded that he knew they had.

As we drove down the hill and turned left toward home, I sat in the back seat and pulled at the elastic of my bonnet, putting it into my mouth and chewing on it carefully.

My mind was crowded with thoughts.

I wondered if Beverly was lonely. I knew I would be. And it was very sad to think that her parents didn't visit her like we had just visited our dead. I wondered if I would be able to come back and play with Beverly and if she would ever be able to leave her grave and venture farther away so we could have a good time together. I wondered if she would ever be able to come to my home and play with me after her parents came back to visit her. I wondered how Grandma knew that the dead had enjoyed our visit—none of them except the dead man whose grave I stepped on and Beverly seemed to have come and said anything at all. I didn't think that my grand-parents were able to talk to the dead like I was, and I wasn't about to ask them.

I was silent and, as always, kept my thoughts to myself.

We did return to the cemetery in the fall to collect the containers for the flowers and to tend to the graves, but Beverly never came to visit me again. I hoped that she had maybe gone to Heaven and had lots of angels for friends or maybe even Emmie had come and taken her to the big meadow to play with all the other children.

The ritual of visiting the dead at the cemetery was to continue for me. My grandparents both encouraged me before they died to keep up the practice, which I do to this day. Because Beverly's grave always seems so vacant and lonely, I often bring flowers to place there and pause to send her a silent prayer in case she is able to hear me.

On Memorial Day weekend of 2011, my husband and I went to the cemetery to place flowers on the graves. When we walked across the road to Beverly's grave I paused and then placed a potted pink geranium in front of her stone. As I stepped back to take a photo of the grave—and despite it being a warm day with no breezes moving through the place—a sudden burst of icy cold air whirled around my feet, and I heard the sound of a young girl's voice in front of me say "Ahhhh" with a heavy yet contented sigh. It was as though Beverly knew I was there, and she was now at peace because she had not been forgotten.

And so my later years found me learning so much more about the real life that awaited all of us on the other side of death's door, and my teachers would be those who had already crossed the boundary.

The dead were ready to teach me, and I was very willing to learn.

chapter three

My Beloved Grandparents

My grandfather was deeply inspired by the lore of his Irish homeland and an avid believer in all things ghostly. Having been close to death both personally and professionally as a gravedigger in Ireland, he viewed dying as no more than a simple leaving of the spirit from the body and that spirit moving on to a place he believed was Heaven.

As I noted, both of my grandparents passed away when I was just eighteen and within five months of one another. Just prior to his death in February of 1970, my grandfather told me that he was going to leave Pleasant View to me. While he was talking to me he put his hands on my shoulders, looked me in the eyes, and said quite calmly and lovingly that he would be back after his death to "check" on me and make sure I was all right. He admonished me that I should not ever be scared if I felt him or Grandma about the house in spirit form.

Grandma and Grandpa McNally on the front lawn
at Pleasant View, in about 1964

With the naiveté of a young girl I heard his words, but I did not want to take them to heart. He would, I believed and hoped, stay with me for a very long time and live to see me graduate from college and even beyond. We would form a deep relationship of mutual respect and trust. We would be able to once more have a garden and maybe some baby chicks. Perhaps we could travel to distant places. He had always wanted to return to Ireland, and at the urging of a neighbor family he went to a travel agency and began looking into fares and trip information to that magical land of his birth.

About a week after his talk with me, Grandpa began a massive renovation of Pleasant View, starting in the basement with all-new plumbing, a new furnace, and new pipes. Upstairs he re-wallpapered, painted, and put down new linoleum and several new windows. He told me that he was getting Pleasant View ready for me to take ownership and that he didn't think I would need to be burdened with upkeep after his passing.

A few weeks after this he died of a heart attack while on his way to a doctor's appointment.

The crushing blow of losing both of the people who had nurtured me from infancy to college age was beyond painful, and I would grieve his loss on and off for many years. Yet in the face of the initial shock of his death I recalled not only all the things I'd learned as a child but also Grandpa's serene attitude about death. "It's just a going to sleep in one place and waking up in another," he had always said. So, in the turmoil of finding myself pretty much alone in the world, I clung to his words—to the knowing in my heart that the absence of his physical form did not mean either he or Grandma were really *gone*.

Sure enough, and as if to prove the validity of the marvelous ghostly tales he had told me when I was a child, Grandpa kept his promise and returned. This first return was as a voice in my mind to help me locate a security box he had told me about just weeks before he died. The box contained all of his important legal papers, and he had instructed me, as soon as I heard of his passing, to take it to the bank that was the executor of his estate. The only problem was that he had neglected to tell me where he kept the box.

It was the day after Grandpa had died and I was at the house with one of my college boyfriends. We had looked everywhere for the box and had been totally unsuccessful. Finally, I called a halt to the dashing about and stood in the center of the kitchen floor and summoned Grandpa with my mind. I never doubted that he would return to help, because he had told me that if I ever needed him after he died all I had to do was call him and he would be there as soon as he could.

Sure enough, within seconds of my mental summons, there was a hint of cigarette smoke and newly mown grass accompanied by a cool breeze close to the right side of my face. Grandpa's voice whispered in my mind telling me where to look for the box. My boyfriend was standing nearby, a bit unsure of exactly what I was doing, but, nevertheless, accepting. I told him the spot Grandpa had indicated. He climbed to it and there was the box—just as Grandpa had directed.

Silently, I thanked Grandpa for his help, and the scents that would become forever associated with his spirit faded away. A short while later the box was delivered to the bank.

Back at college and a few weeks after Grandpa's funeral I suffered terribly from panic attacks. It was the most horrible and crippling sensation that came over me without warning and spiraled me into a realm of unimaginable terror. I felt so totally out of control, adrift and alone, despite my boyfriend's love and care. I had lost both of my anchors, and my body and soul now seemed to exist on two separate levels of being. Other things also had changed—things that most teenagers took for granted. I remember vividly that when the first college holiday break came I had no home to go to. Once I went reluctantly with my boyfriend to his parents' home near Buffalo, New York, still dealing with the anxiety and sense of displacement. Once, during a long weekend break at college, I was allowed to stay in my dorm room because I truly had no place to go to—no neighbors or family or friends seemed to want to be burdened with my presence. I remember how powerfully lonely it was to be the only one in the entire dorm. No voices and no sounds, only the occasional custodian cleaning or a security guard to check on me.

Yet, again, despite the love and support of my college mates, I was, for all intents and purposes, an orphan.

The estate executors met me at the house several weeks after Grandpa's death, and while they did a quick inventory of the contents of Pleasant View I packed up the things I would need for the next few months or longer. A locksmith arrived, and all the locks on the doors were changed. The executors took the keys with them. I was not given a key and would not be allowed admittance until the will was probated, and then I would only be allowed into my own home if a lawyer or trustee was with me.

Now I was also homeless.

I know that Grandpa must have grown very concerned for my well-being, because about three months after his passing he paid me a first dream visit.

I was in my college dorm room. I remember waking up quickly and glancing bleary-eyed at the ticking Baby Ben alarm clock on my bedside table. The hands showed it was 2:45 a.m. I don't know what had awakened me, so after looking around the room and seeing that all was as it should be, I lay back down and went into a deep sleep.

I immediately began to dream.

In the dream I found I was able to fly quite easily and that I was following along the path of a stream that ran next to a row of green-leafed trees and a sunlit meadow. Birds of all sorts were winging past me and didn't seem too concerned about seeing me gliding along their flight paths. I turned my light-as-air body to the left and flew over the meadow and willed my dream self to go lower so that I could skim the meadow.

I watched as rabbits hopped along through the grass. In another field nearby deer grazed peacefully. Butterflies floated on unseen currents of air. As I glanced down I saw that there were many families and groups of people picnicking. Near these families were dogs and cats resting on blankets or chasing one another playfully through the vast field. The blankets or quilts were of every hue and color. Next to each family or group was an open-topped wooden picnic basket loaded with sandwiches and other foodstuffs wrapped in waxed paper or boxed. Beside the baskets were bottles of soda, jugs of iced tea, water, or lemonade. However, I noticed that no one was either drinking or eating. There was also the sound of many conversations and laughter and children shrieking with joy, yet not one person's mouth moved.

It was all so familiar from my "Emmie" days at the hospital.

I felt pulled along as if by an energy force to the farther end of the field and kept on a straight flight path.

I looked down and there was Grandpa! Physically he appeared about the same as he had when he had been alive and thus was easily recognizable. He was even wearing the gray double-breasted suit he had been buried in. On the blanket next to him was a much younger-looking Grandma, and I was able to recognize her from photos I had seen of her when she was in her early thirties. Also on the blanket was a blond-haired boy playing patty cake with two toddler girls who mentally giggled with joy. These I recognized as Edward Junior, age nine when he had died, and I guessed that the two little girls were his lost sisters, Cathleen Dora and Gene Ann, both about age two when they had passed and now the same age here.

Grandpa and Grandma shaded their eyes and looked up at me and waved. Grandpa shouted to me with his mind, "Don't you worry about me. I'm doing fine. You go on back to your studies and get your mind off this. You're going to be all right."

I waved at them and circled them a few times and then headed back over the treetops.

The next thing I knew I was waking up in my dorm room and the springtime dawn was breaking and glints of sunshine were coming in through the window.

I sat up in bed and thought about the dream. It had been so real. I had actually felt the warm rays of the sun on my back as I had flown along. I had heard the lapping of the water against the rocks and smelled the sweet meadow grass. I recalled the freedom of being able to fly and soar with the birds, and I smiled at the memory.

And from this day onward, all my interactions with the dead in my dreams would be filled with the incredible details of sight, sound, and the aromas of the places they took me to. This was again proof that I was not dreaming ordinary dreams, but was indeed a part of something incredibly grand and very beautiful.

This communication by dream visitation was quite new, and I was still unused to the dead coming to me in this manner, but I had to admit it had been wonderful to see my dearly loved and much-missed grandparents together and happy with their children beside them. Also, the dream visit had done me a world of good. Over the next few months the anxiety subsided and only flared up occasionally. I credit my boyfriend's tender care and concern and the knowledge that my grandparents truly worried about me and were not that far away if I needed them.

Because of my grandparents' dream visit to me I began to heal somewhat and then to embrace the tentative first stages of letting go of the past and reaching for my own future. It was a very painful process.

Several years would pass before Grandpa returned in spirit. During those years from eighteen to twenty-three, much would change in my life, but my grandparents were ever vigilant. My grandfather continued to make certain that he kept his promise to return to me after he died, and he was constantly close whenever I needed his strength to lean on during any rough times. Likewise, my grandmother did the same.

Grandpa's First Ghostly Visit

At age twenty-one I came into legal ownership of my childhood home. During the time shortly after the deed to the property passed into my hands, I had come to a sort of uneasy peace about the house. On a few occasions I had gone to Pleasant View just to sit and ponder the total emptiness of the place—an emptiness that echoed in my heart. I cleaned and cared minimally for the little bungalow, learning acceptance of my lost childhood spent within the sweet, dear walls.

Echoes surrounded me at every corner. Bits of the three lives that had loved and cherished one another were found in every nook and cranny and caused sobs to rise up in my throat constantly. There, hanging on a nail in the cellar, was the carpenter's apron Grandpa had worn while renovating the house—with the nails still in the pockets. There in the cupboard was his white ceramic coffee cup. Grandma's homemade aprons hung on a hook by the cellar door as if waiting for her to come into the room, put one on, and begin getting dinner ready. Their chairs still sat side by side in the kitchen, in the space where the comforting kitchen woodstove had once been. In the bedroom their beds still awaited, the bedcovers smooth and ready.

I pondered deeply how it was that the little things a person leaves behind when they depart this world could cut so deeply into the heart of one left behind.

My yearning for all the lost yesterdays—all the time taken for granted, all the "I love you"s left unsaid and hugs not given—brought unendurable sorrow, and I realized that, on some level, my sorrow was now a part of the fiber of the yearning I had sensed in Pleasant View when I had been a young girl.

The yearning forged a link with the home that would be unbreakable.

Time passed.

In the intervening years my college boyfriend and I went our separate ways after he was drafted and enlisted in the Navy. I met and fell in love with the man who would become my first husband, and we moved in together and made plans to get married.

One day he informed me that his parents were coming to pay a visit, and out of respect for them I decided that I would go to stay overnight at Pleasant View. I took along my gray tabby cat, Muffin, for company.

Entering the house on that autumn afternoon was like entering a crypt.

The house had stood empty for a while and I had only come by sporadically to clean it. The furnace no longer worked so I made do with a little portable space heater that I set up in the living room. All around me were the spiritual echoes of loving voices, laughter long stilled, and faint reverberations of my own child self that seemed to wander lost through every room searching for a time that would be no more.

The aroma of age clung to the place—a musty, nearly dank mildew scent that, while not pleasant, was also not totally disagreeable.

I put Muffin down, set up her litter box and food dishes in the kitchen, and turned on the heater and then the old console TV for company. I cleaned and scrubbed for a while and then fixed a dinner of canned peas on the stove that only had one working burner. I sat down on the floor in front of the sofa and drank hot tea and ate a ham and cheese sandwich and some of the peas, while Muffin begged now and then for a few peas of her own as appetizers. As darkness began to close in around us I made up my bed on the foldout sofa, got into my night clothes, and climbed under the blankets. Muffin sat beside me grooming herself.

Darkness tiptoed across the land, and as the temperature outside dropped into the forties the house began to creak and moan as it settled into the night. Unused to the sounds and to being totally alone in Pleasant View for the first time in my life, I flinched at every noise. I remembered that I had no phone connection to the outside world and was thus effectively cut off from communication.

The lamps were off, the little space heater hummed, and the coils cast a red-orange hue to the room. It would come on and shut off through the night, recycling itself as it adjusted to the temperature changes. On the television was a black-and-white movie starring Boris Karloff, he of horror-film fame.

I left the TV on, covered up my head with my blanket, and went to sleep. An hour or so later I was awakened by the fizzing sound of the now-shutdown TV station. I got up and turned off the set.

The silence was deafening, and with the little heater cycled off, the darkness was deep for a few minutes.

When the heater came back on I reached out for Muffin, who had moved to sit on the sofa arm at the foot of my bed. I attempted to draw her close to me and put her under the covers, but she would have none of it. In fact, she began growling softly and hissing. I looked at her and saw she was puffed up in fear and her eyes were fixated on the doorway to what once was my grandparents' bedroom. I squinted my eyes, and it seemed to me that a transparent lighter shadow was overlaying the doorway darkness. The lighter shadow began to move slowly toward me.

Muffin had moved behind me and had flattened herself against the wall. She gave one last growl and hiss and ran off under a table.

Suddenly, the temperature in the room dropped enough so that I noticed it. I drew the covers around me. The little heater was humming busily away.

Then came the familiar aroma of cigarette smoke and newly mown grass, and I relaxed.

I sat on the edge of the sofa and waited.

The space heater turned off and the room was plunged into total darkness, yet I felt no fear.

Softly and tenderly came the tentative icy cold touch of individual fingers running along the back of my neck. The feeling was not unlike having both an ice cube and static electricity graze across my skin.

I did not flinch from the contact, as I knew in my heart that it was Grandpa doing the best he could to reassure me of his very real presence.

"Hello, Grandpa," I said aloud. "I miss you, too. Thank you for coming to visit, but everything's okay. I'm just here for the night."

Immediately, the caress ceased and the aromas associated with Grandpa began to fade.

After this visitation, there was a very deep silence in the house, as if by coming to visit me Grandpa had used up an inordinate amount of energy.

The space heater again came back on, filling the room with warmth and light. Muffin eased carefully out of her hiding place and got under the blankets with me, and I fell asleep knowing that Grandpa was somewhere nearby watching over me as he always done since my infancy.

At the time of this visit to me, Grandpa had been in spirit for about four years.

As time passed there were often hints of Grandpa's presence. Sometimes I would enter a room at Pleasant View and there was the comforting aroma of cigarette smoke and newly mown grass swirling about almost as if he had exited just ahead of me. There would be quick rustling noises from the kitchen area at night that were very similar to the ones Grandpa had made when seated on his chair by the kitchen woodstove reading his newspaper or turning the pages of a library book.

I had several dreams of Grandpa in the early 1990s to mid-2000s, and these mostly involved my journeys back in time to my schoolgirl days when I was living with my grandparents at Pleasant View. These forays into the past usually seemed to involve me arriving home on the school bus and having the bus stop a ways up the road from the house instead of directly in front as it had done when I was a student. It would always be nightfall in the dream, and I would be hesitant about approaching Pleasant View even though it had welcoming lights shining out of every window. The one thing I consistently noted was that the little bungalow had altered its exterior appearance back to the way it had been when I was young.

I would walk up to the front door and either wait and listen for any sounds from within or go boldly in. If I waited outside I somehow was able to sense what was going on within. Often I felt that my grandparents were home but somehow *unavailable*. If I went in without knocking, the house was as it was in design and furnishings as it had appeared in years past. Sometimes in these dreams Grandpa would answer the door and look at me as if I were a stranger. He still appeared the same physically as he had just before he had passed away.

The fact that he didn't recognize me was something easily explained away. I had, by the time of these dreams, aged into my forties and fifties and time had passed, altering my own physical appearance. Perhaps the confusion came for him because he expected a younger version of me to be standing in front of him. These dreams were both comforting and upsetting, because it created in my heart and soul a longing for another time and place. Thankfully, these dream journeys back to my youth ended abruptly and all was relatively quiet for a while. Somehow I sensed Grandpa was now resting and attempting to come to terms with his status in the afterlife.

An Unusual Heavenly Place

My grandparents were to reappear in 1984 during a near-death experience I had after my car accident. Then a long silence descended until 2009.

Again I fell into a deep slumber and immediately sensed Grandpa's presence. The dream was vivid with the usual details of sight, sound, and smell.

I found myself in a large room that smelled of disinfectant and other hospital-like aromas. At first the exact nature of what the place was remained unknown to me until gradually it seemed to light itself from inside with a glowing white light. Ever so slowly, things began to take form and shape, and I realized I was standing in a corridor of some kind near a nurses' station. Though it appeared to be nighttime it didn't feel like it was—it seemed as if this place I was in was suspended in a time between time. To my right and past the nurses' station were several long glass windows that looked out on a vista of millions of twinkling stars set in a dark sky. There was a discomfiting sensation that whatever this place was it was not anchored to any earthly space, but rather somehow floating in an ethereal dimension far beyond Earth.

In front of me were three steps up to an open area and another hallway. The floor that stretched out before me was white linoleum, and it glowed with a sheen that almost hurt my eyes. Branching ahead of me was another corridor that stretched into an unfathomable distance and was alternately in light and in shadow. Around me were many nurses and orderlies who seemed to be hurrying past on urgent business. These people had no cognizance of my presence and did not seem to care that I was in their way—in fact, most of them simply moved through me, making my body tingle with a feeling that tiny amounts of electricity were briefly rearranging my molecules. They all wore glowing white uniforms very reminiscent of those worn by medical personnel at hospitals for the living.

I kept glancing at the three steps before me and found I really did not want to even go up any of them.

Soon I knew I had to make a move, and so I took a deep breath and put my foot on the bottom step.

Quite suddenly Grandpa was there standing on the top step. He was dressed in his familiar everyday clothes of tan slacks, brown belt, tan cap, and a red, white, and green checked flannel shirt. He still physically appeared to be about age eighty, the age he had been when he had passed. He looked down at me with kindness and love radiating from his face. His piercing gray-blue eyes twinkled despite the creases and wrinkles time had etched on his countenance. I noticed that on the left side of his face there was now clearly visible the large scar from the time he'd had a cancerous tumor removed and skin had been grafted over the spot.

He spoke to me in my mind.

"Well, Johnny, here we are again."

He hadn't called me Johnny since I was eighteen, and I felt it as an endearing gesture. I listened to him as he continued.

"Now I don't want you to worry about me anymore. I'm getting younger and stronger every minute. Just watch this."

Around me the room went quiet as all the nurses and orderlies paused to watch Grandpa. There was an expectant hush as we all turned our attention to him.

Right before my eyes he did begin to grow younger, as if some remarkable and miraculous time-erasing intervention was going on inside his being. His face became wrinkle-free. The horrible surgical scar vanished to be replaced by smooth, healthy-looking skin. His body straightened. His hair went from snowy white to brown. He seemed to gain a bit of weight and filled out, health and peace radiating from his entire person. No longer frail and ill in appearance, he now looked as he had in the photos I had seen of him and Grandma when they had first married in their thirties.

When the transformation was complete, he sighed with satisfaction and smiled at me.

But now he was silent.

A nurse came up to me. She was a short, heavyset woman with curly brown hair; a friendly, comforting smile; and soothing brown eyes. She was bubbling over with joy and she seemed particularly proud of Grandpa's recent transformation. She patted him on the arm and turned to me and mind-talked.

"Okay, your grandpa is all better and ready for the next phase of his journey." She paused and looked at me closely as if trying to fathom how I was going to react to her next words. "You'll have to say goodbye to him for a while, but don't worry. He'll be around if you really need him, but he has a great deal of work yet to do and will be very busy."

I knew this was it.

I wondered if I would be allowed to hug Grandpa goodbye.

As if divining my thoughts, the nurse nodded. "You may hug him, but be quick. He's forming fully into spirit."

I grasped Grandpa's hands in mine. I went fearlessly up to the top step, and he pulled me into an embrace that poured joy and hope and love into my being. Then he quickly released me, turned, and walked off across the glowing white floor and headed down the light-and-shadow corridor. There I could clearly see my young-appearing grandmother waiting, and she turned and blew me a kiss as she put her arm through Grandpa's arm. For the briefest of moments, a magnificently bright white light surrounded both of them as they moved down the corridor and vanished from my sight. At their leave-taking the entire area was now quiet again. No more nurses and orderlies rushed about. It was as if Grandpa's transformation had been a trigger for it all to end. The light faded, and all I could see were the stars twinkling through the windows.

At the time of this dream, Grandpa had been in spirit for almost forty years and I had the sense that he had moved on to a higher level of learning on the other side of death's door.

My grandfather had always been a man of his word.

He had more than kept his promise to me to watch over me despite no longer being in physical form. And, to this day, I know that he is not that far away and that he will come to me as quickly as he can to watch over me—to love, protect, and comfort me.

I miss him and Grandma every day but know that they are both doing fine.

Marilou and her grandmother, circa 1955

Grandma

My sweet grandmother passed on when she was in her eighties in September of 1969. For the last ten years of her life whenever I had asked her how old she was on her birthday she always said without hesitation, "Sixty-five." I caught on to her by the third year when I again asked her the question and got the same answer. That time she added, "That is my age, and it isn't changing."

I always felt she was onto something good, but that didn't stop me from asking her the age question every year.

I recall a deeply revealing and interesting conversation I had with Grandma during the last summer she spent on Earth.

Darkness had fallen around Pleasant View. Outside the kitchen screen door and open windows the crickets were chirping and warm breezes whispered through the trees. The scent of the garden sweet corn drifted down into the room. All was peaceful.

That particular evening I had the overwhelming urge to revert to my childhood self and sit on Grandma's lap and have her read me my very favorite children's books, *The Party Pig* and *The Little Red Hen*. I was eighteen and very slim. I eased myself onto her lap as she sat on her favorite chair in the kitchen.

It must be related that I had known for some time that she would not be with us much longer. Her once-robust frame was slimmer, her movements were slower, and small chores seemed to sap her strength. She was fading before my eyes, and despite the fact that she was still physically present I was missing her already.

Also, a few months before this night and a couple of weeks before my high school graduation, I'd had a dream of premonition about her death. I had told no one about this dream but my first boyfriend, Butch, who had driven the ninety or so miles from his home to take me to my senior prom and to be with me for my graduation day. He had listened intently as he sat with me in the front seat of his car, keeping his arm around me the whole time as I choked back my fear and my tears. He had been an excellent sounding board for these talks, because he never judged and he was never fazed by the content of any of my vivid dreams.

After I had gotten it all out he simply said, "Well, babe, it's very sad, but if it's true what you dreamed, then it probably means that your grandmother is going to die soon and you are being prepared for it. There isn't much you can do about it, you know. People die when it's time for them to go."

Cut to the chase, that was Butch.

Then he held me close against him, and I nestled my head on his shoulder as he quietly consoled me.

The morning of my graduation I noticed that Grandma was very listless. She held her left hand at an angle that wasn't natural, and in the later photos taken of her that day she was standing with her eyes closed, her hands limp, and her face slack.

That whole warm June day the dark essence of the dream insinuated itself into my mind during every part of the graduation ceremony.

It was like waiting for the proverbial next shoe to fall.

After it was all over and Butch had gone home, I was once more alone with my grandparents.

I watched and worried as Grandma seemed to fall asleep in her chair in the kitchen more than usual. She began to forget things. She would put a kettle or a cooking pot with vegetables in it on the stove and not remember it until the smell of burning food or metal made Grandpa and me afraid she would burn the house down. For safety's sake, Grandpa removed the knobs from the stove and kept them in his pocket. My grandmother cried piteously when this was done, as it meant a loss of control over things she had done all her life and taken for granted. Grandpa and I would either have to supervise her or make whatever was for lunch or dinner.

So when I climbed on her lap on that summer night in 1969 and snuggled against her talcum-powdered neck that smelled of flowers and warmth, I tried very hard to memorize her dear voice as she read my favorite stories to me twice. I tried to memorize her soft Southern accent, her calling me "honey child," and her soft kisses on my face after the books were closed.

Grandpa was seated nearby reading a library book and having his evening cup of hot tea. I climbed down onto a small chair beside Grandma. To this day I don't know why I felt compelled to talk to her about death but the subject rose up in my mind with a great urgency, and with the impetuousness of youth I asked, "Grandma, when I die will you wait for me?"

She looked down at me with something akin to relief in her gray eyes.

She reached out and took my hand in her softly wrinkled one and then moved her hand to tuck it under my chin and look at me closely. "Of course I'll wait for you, child. I will never leave you. I'll be right there when your time comes. I'll be there to get you."

I leaned against her side and then laid my head on her lap as she stroked my hair gently, almost lulling me to sleep. After a while Grandpa got up and rinsed out his teacup in the sink, put his glasses back in their case, and declared that it was time for bed.

My precognitive dream of Grandma's death became a reality that September, when I was just about two weeks into my college year. She'd had a stroke at the beginning of the month, just as I was getting ready to leave for a weekend visit with Butch and his family before heading off to college in Delhi, New York, about a half-hour away from my home.

Grandpa relied on me to get him through a great deal of the arrangements, and we went together to pick out a casket at the funeral home. We found one lined with pale yellow satin and thought it sunshiny and nice. We bypassed all the funerary attire for sale and opted to have Grandma buried in the blue-rose dress we had gotten her for Mother's Day that year.

At the funeral home for the wake I kept a close eye on Grandpa, who seemed so lost. I also spent a great deal of time watching Grandma as she lay in her casket. She looked so peaceful lying there with her hands folded and her eyes closed and her glasses on. It was her hands that lay so still and unusually quiet that bothered me the most. Those hands had comforted me when I was ill, caressed me into sleep during fitful nights, and held me close when I was afraid. Now so still. I remember I put my hands atop her too-cold ones and cried. I so badly wanted her to open her eyes and wake up from this eternal nap.

But of course she couldn't.

Eventually I went to sit on a chair in the next room that was tucked into a corner. From this angle I had full view of the casket and could just make out the tip of Grandma's nose.

Grandpa came by, touched me gently on the head, and went up to kneel by the casket, spending his last moments with the woman who had been his best friend.

I glanced at him and then blinked several times in awe.

Grandma was standing at the head of the casket and she was looking down at Grandpa with incredible love—and then she looked up at me!

She was dressed in the Mother's Day dress and I could see right through her to the sheer curtains of the window behind her. Her eyes seemed so sad as she watched Grandpa kneeling there.

I wanted so badly to go over to her but something kept me in my place.

She reached out to Grandpa and then withdrew her hand as he made the sign of the cross, stood up, and left the room.

Grandma lingered for a few seconds more, then she smiled at me and vanished.

I knew then that she was okay, but that she was very lonely for Grandpa.

I kept her visit to myself for a while, but when Butch and his mother arrived for the funeral and the gathering at Pleasant View afterward and he and I got a chance to be alone and take a long walk away from all the "grown-ups," I told him about Grandma's spectral visit.

He paused as we walked through an autumn field next to the Susquehanna River, and he put his hands on my shoulders. "You're very lucky to be able to see your grandmother like that and know she's okay."

He pulled me into a loving hug and held me close for a very long time. Then he took my hand, and we continued walking and allowed our too-brief time together to help me heal.

After everyone had left that day and all the food had been put away, Grandpa went into deep grieving. He sat for hours on his chair by the chimney in the kitchen where once the kitchen woodstove had been, and he kept crying and saying over and over again, "I've lost my best friend."

It was heart-wrenching to see my grandfather like this. I felt so helpless, and I consoled him as well as I could before I had to return to college.

Sadly, it was also during that dark and devastating time that I found out the ones I had counted on to support me were only fair-weather friends. It was a bitter discovery, but despite it all I came through, leaning on Butch, who, even though we had parted ways, kept me on track and going forward with his phone calls and letters.

It wasn't until Grandma had been gone for a month that she paid me a quick visit—well, not exactly a visit, more like one of those mental shouts, and one that shook me to the core.

Walking across the college campus with my new boyfriend, I stopped abruptly as my grandmother's voice echoed in my mind, "I want your grandfather with me! I miss him so!"

Recovering from the words, I continued shakily forward and told my boyfriend about the voice. He was very soothing and calming.

That night, in my dorm room, came the faintest hint of Grandma's Cashmere Bouquet talcum powder, the scent forever connected to her presence in life as it would be after her death. I fell asleep comforted by the oh-so-familiar aroma, but also very scared for the future of my grandfather.

Almost four months to the day of that mental shout, Grandpa died.

I could not say that Grandma hadn't warned me of what was to come.

After Grandpa's death, Grandma didn't visit me again until about five years later, when I was very ill with strep throat and bronchitis. In fact, all of the visits she paid me after 1970 were centered around times when I was ill—but again this makes perfect sense, as she was always nursing me back to health and being very concerned for my well-being after my bout with pneumonia and later asthma.

This dream/form visit while I was ill in the mid-1970s happened while I was caring for my very young niece and nephew.

I had gone to the emergency room and been given antibiotics. I was also plagued with laryngitis. I somehow managed to care for the children, get them ready for bed, and then take my dose of medicine somewhere around nine that night. I crawled into bed and fell asleep from exhaustion almost instantly.

I began to dream but in a way that made it seem as though I was really awake—very different and yet comforting.

The first thing that happened was that the scent of Grandma's talcum powder filled the bedroom. I saw Grandma standing next to my bed and looking down at me. She had not exactly youthened, but she appeared more vibrant and as she had during my growing-up years, when she had been sturdy and full of energy. She was wearing her maroon and gold-brown square-print housedress with one of her homemade long aprons over it.

I was so glad to see her.

She looked down at me with such love in her eyes and then began singing in my mind one of her favorite hymns, "Rock of Ages." Many were the nights when I had been ill or restless as a child that she had sung this to me.

Her sweet trembly voice echoed softly in my head, and I watched as her hand came down to rest tenderly on my forehead.

The next thing I knew the sun was shining in my window and it was morning.

I awoke fully expecting to see Grandma seated next to my bed, which was her usual spot when I was ill.

But of course she wasn't there.

There was the faintest trace of Cashmere Bouquet in the air.

I would only see my grandmother on a couple of other occasions over the years—during dream visits from Grandpa, during my last near-death experience in 1984, and most recently when I was very ill in December of 2010.

Each of these visits brought me great comfort and peace and helped me heal all the more rapidly because I knew that Grandma was still there, still nearby, and still very concerned about my well-being.

chapter four

True Love Never Dies

Ah, the joy of falling in love for the first time! Everything is new and exciting, and if the feelings are real and true it is assured that this is the relationship that will carve pathways through the soul that are everlasting.

Such was my experience when I first met Butch on a gloriously sunny and warm September day in 1967 during my sixteenth year and Butch's fifteenth. Butch was tall and slim with brown, wavy hair and brown eyes that sparkled with delight about every single one of life's possibilities. He had the most engaging lopsided grin that melted my young heart in ways that have never been duplicated. On this day of our meeting he was impeccably dressed in a pale yellow short-sleeved shirt, perfectly creased tan slacks, and shiny brown loafers.

Butch was a blend of controlled recklessness and quiet contemplation. To me he was an intoxicating being who always seemed to be rushing just ahead of me, grabbing life

Butch before the prom, June 1969

into his embrace and not being too concerned about the consequences to himself.

About others whom he loved he was fiercely loyal, loving, and protective. He never failed to speak his mind, and he lived by several mottoes, two of which echo strongly in my mind: "Don't ever let anyone tell you how to live your life" and "Don't do anything to someone else that you don't want done to you, because what goes around comes around."

I know now that Butch came into my life at precisely the right time, and, looking back, I recognize that on quite a few levels he was the other part of me that had been missing. He was a kind and true friend—a companion on the journey and the only person in the world I really trusted and told all my most secret thoughts to, as he did to me. Butch's advice was always solid and cut-to-the-chase, and he understood me and my fears and longings, my dreams and desires, better than I understood them myself. He believed in me totally and I in him. He had no patience with artifice and meaningless words or people who set out to harm another. He had no tolerance for gossip, greed, or jealousy. He abhorred liars and ostentatious persons. He loved a good joke and he drew cartoons with great skill. In a letter to me in October 1967 he devised a code so that "no one can read our letters except us and whoever we want." His method was to use the alphabet and number the letters backwards (so that the letter *z* became a number *1* and so forth). We had a tough time decoding one of those letters—but lots of fun fooling the "grown-ups."

When one of my girlfriends began to make fun of me for having a boyfriend who lived so far away, I immediately was very hurt and told Butch about it in a letter. Ever protective of me, his response as he was closing the letter was, "What's this? What did she say about you? Forget it. She's just jealous." Butch was always direct and always right.

When Butch and I first met, we discovered that we lived about an hour or so apart, and as neither of us had driver's licenses, the distance between us seemed a vast, uncharted dark zone and the time between our visits felt as if it stretched into eternity. We communicated via voluminous letters and we both looked forward to our allotted fifteen-minute biweekly telephone calls. When Butch finally got his license he would often drive up to see me without the knowledge of some of his relatives. He had a beautiful white Plymouth Fury convertible with a blue interior. During that second summer together we rode the backcountry roads near my home with the top down and the radio blasting our favorite songs: "Incense and Peppermints" by the Strawberry Alarm Clock, "The Rain, the Park & Other Things" by the Cowsills, and "Cherish" by the Association, a song that would sadly become a sort of theme for our relationship.

Oh! Life was so good it could almost be tasted!

Sometimes our relationship seemed as if it were on fast forward and that we had so much catching up to do before the time for us to be together ended. There was a sort of peculiar urgency to those days, and we tried to cram as much into being friends as possible. I know that we both felt this quick turning-over of the days on some level—we both heard the invisible clock ticking off the hours, minutes, and seconds of our lives, but we chose to ignore it and live for the moment. Our love was a pure one of delight in one another and in enjoying to the full the days that we hoped we had. I call that time with Butch *ethereal* because the fabric of those precious moments seemed made of some fine and gossamer thing that was strong, yet also fragile. We never attempted a physical relationship beyond holding hands and sharing a few quick and soft kisses of innocent joy and discovery. We lived for one another to be happy and safe with the other.

I recall that Butch didn't really deal too well with change. So I always knew to break things to him gently. However, in the late spring of 1968 I made the decision to have my very long hair cut into what was then called a "boy cut"—or very short hair.

I had told Butch about the hair appointment but hadn't told him the total story, as I knew it would probably upset him. So Butch found out what I'd done when I sent him a newspaper photo of me taken in my high school courtyard, where I was gathered with a group of my classmates who, like me, had just received scholastic awards. His words in a letter to me after receiving the photo tell it all: "When you said a haircut I thought you meant an inch off all the way around. I hate short hair but you look so *sharp* with short hair I could squeeze ya to death! ... I LOVE YOUR SHORT HAIR NO MATTER WHAT ANYONE SAYS!! I'M GOING TO SHOW EVERYONE MARILOU—THE NEAT, SHORT HAIRED, SHARP, SWEET COOL CAT KID FROM ONEONTA!!!"

This letter seemed to be one in which Butch began to delve deeply into his maturing feelings for me. There were promises of the joyful days that lay ahead for us. He was full of apologies for being behind in his letter-writing and couldn't wait for some time when we could be alone to discuss the future of our relationship—a discussion he dearly wanted to be devoid of all grown-ups and youngsters—and thankfully that did happen, but only with a bit of eluding of the various said grown-ups and youngsters who seemed to attach themselves to us.

In my later years I would define Butch as an "old soul"— a being whose spiritual development was remarkably advanced and who required only an infinitesimal bit of life experience on the earth plane in order to return to his heavenly home for good.

To me, Butch was an angel—my very own special angel —and even after our relationship broke off when I went away to college, I always knew that he would be there for me if I really needed him. Somehow we had become a part of one another for eternity.

As our teen years passed and we moved into our twenties, we still maintained sporadic contact despite all the ins and outs of growing up. When my grandparents died, Butch was with me both times—consoling, touching, holding, and grounding me. His support and love and concern were ever constant.

He also never let me forget the joy of those early days, and so the bond that had first formed during the beginning of being together remained strong. We were both thankful for the love we had formed because we knew that it was made up of powerful emotions and deep regard not granted to many mortals.

Little did I know that the deep and everlasting bond we had formed would come to mean so much more to me than I had ever imagined.

A few years after my college days ended, Butch and I lost contact as life moved forward in different directions for both of us. For me there was coming into ownership of Pleasant View, a first marriage, a divorce, work, writing, and raising my niece and nephew. During those years I moved further and further away into a fragmented life that gradually seemed to cut me off from the carefree person I had been when Butch and I were young and together. I was often kept up to date on his life progress and heard from various people that he had gone to law school, and been employed in a trendy Manhattan hairstyling salon where he was lauded in a book as one of the stylists Jacqueline Kennedy Onassis preferred.

One day in mid-July of 1990, toward the late afternoon, I began to feel quite lethargic, as if something was draining the energy from my soul. I went to my bedroom and lay down for a nap. I immediately fell into an incredibly deep slumber.

Little did I know that Butch and I were about to be reunited and in a way I never wanted to have happen.

In the dream I found myself walking along a sunlit and tree-lined dirt road in a deeply forested area. It was summertime and I could hear the birds singing, smell the scent of pine and dirt, hear the crunch of twigs and dead leaves beneath my feet, and feel the rush of cooling breezes on my face and in my hair.

As I walked along I got the overwhelming feeling that I was here to meet someone, but I had no idea who that someone might be.

I stopped and looked up the road.

A short distance away, on the left side of the road, I could vaguely make out a figure sitting on the ground beneath the shade of a giant oak tree. I walked closer and stopped. It was a young man, about thirty or so. He had dark-brown wavy hair, brown eyes that assessed me carefully, and a lopsided grin. He was wearing a pale yellow cashmere sweater, a white shirt open at the collar, tan slacks, and highly polished brown loafers.

This young man looked so familiar and yet—

I moved a bit closer to him and shaded my eyes.

"Hello, Marilou," he said with spoken words. "Fancy meeting you here."

As soon as he spoke I recognized him instantly—it was Butch!

Oh, how I wanted to run to him and hold him, but something that felt like an invisible force field held me back. He remained seated beneath the tree and patted the ground beside him, indicating that I should come and sit next to him, which I did.

I watched as he played with a handful of dead pine needles, switching them from hand to hand before letting them slide through his slim fingers and to the ground. He seemed to be weighing his words carefully, glancing at me sideways with great concern.

Then—

"I just died a little while ago and I had to stop for a few minutes to rest. I was hoping you'd come along because I thought you'd like to know what happened to me."

It was odd, but my dream self was not at all shocked by the news of his recent passing. I pondered that on some level I had always known that this day would come and that he would leave the earth plane before me. It also seemed very natural to sit and talk with him in spirit much as we had talked when he was alive. Later I would ponder his inability to mind-talk to me, and I reasoned that perhaps it was because he had so recently died.

I looked up and down the road, but all was peaceful. Butch seemed to want to try to catch up on all the things we had done since we had been apart—at this point in real time almost twenty years had passed since we had last visited with one another at Pleasant View, and we were both nearing our forties. We sat and laughed about the days of our youth when the credo was "Don't trust anyone over thirty" and our favorite word was *groovy*. We also spent a few moments recalling how we wore matching bell-bottom jeans that were so tight we had to lie down on the floor to zip them up—and then, as we couldn't move because the material was so stiff, we had to roll and get leverage on a piece of furniture and pull ourselves to a standing position, where we stood like cardboard cutouts for a while before attempting to move forward like robots as we held on to one another to prevent a fall.

So many joyful memories were shared between us during that dream visit: my prom, the way he had re-fixed my hair after my visit to the beauty salon, tie-dying our jeans with bleach, our extremely long letters to one another written on most any form of paper we could find, from index cards to taped-together tissues to paper towels—and how we had most always miscalculated the postage by a few cents and had to "pay up" to the postman.

Butch also spoke about some of the new feelings he'd had about his family and friends. He said, "It doesn't matter anymore" when talking about his teenaged angst about his parents' divorce. He said, "I've had a good life. I've known love. I wish I could have stayed longer, but all things come to an end and I have to accept that."

With his usual cut-to-the-chase directness he voiced his feelings and moved quickly to acceptance of his present situation just as he had done when he found out that I had radically altered my hairstyle. I admired him for that and for his candor and his sharing his time with me. It was, I knew, a heart-wrenching time for him, yet he was facing it head on and coming to grips with it. I also knew he would be all right in his new life.

Our conversation turned backward to our shared past and all the silly things we had done and the sound of our laughter, and "remember when"s echoed off the trees and seemed to spiral upward to the heavens.

It may seem odd, but I never asked him how he died. It didn't seem to matter.

He did tell me that he'd had a hard time dying, but then he looked at me with those all-knowing brown eyes and said, "But then it really wasn't so bad. You just have to let go and free fall into death and not fight it. You have to trust."

There then came a subtle yet sudden shift in the air and in the light around us, and I knew our time together was coming to a close.

We both stood in unison and brushed the debris off our pants.

"Well, I guess this is it, then," I said. I was already missing him terribly and all over again. "It's goodbye, isn't it?"

Tears pricked at the corners of my eyes, and I brushed them away quickly. He smiled at me with that adorable lopsided grin that made my heart ache. "Not goodbye forever, babe. I'll be away for just a while. This place isn't that far away from where you are, you know. It's just another dimension."

I couldn't resist. I moved up to him for a hug, but he backed away and put up his hand to stop me. "Sorry, babe. We can't touch one another yet. I'm newly in spirit and you're in flesh. Touching me when I'm like this might harm you. I'm not sure how I know that, but I don't want to take any chances."

Tears started flowing from my eyes, dripping onto the roadway. I was ashamed of showing my emotions so easily.

I recalled that I had rarely cried in front of Butch when we were teenagers. Back then I had always wanted to appear braver than I felt. This time the grief of losing him was overwhelming.

I turned and started to walk away.

A few paces from him I sensed that he hadn't moved, so I turned around.

He was still standing in the center of the road and smiling at me tenderly. I noticed that his eyes suddenly seemed lit with a new inner fire that conveyed peacefulness and a knowledge beyond my senses. He seemed to glow with a beautiful golden radiance as if he were taking in all the sunlight and making it his own personal power source. He kept his eyes on mine as he gradually faded and became one with the light that illuminated his form. And then he was gone.

I knew when I awoke that Butch was dead and that he had truly come to me in my dream to tell me of his passing. He was no phantom, no see-through being. His essence surrounded me on that roadway just as it had when we were together all those years ago. I believe that he divined that perhaps I would not be told of his death or maybe I would find out in a cruel way. And so, because I know true love never dies, I know Butch reached out to me from beyond life's door to protect me from pain, to comfort and reassure me. To give me courage. To give me hope. To take away the fear and the dread associated with his physical death.

I had no way of actually knowing via any out-of-town newspapers that Butch had died on that July day, and I was not, at that time, in contact with any of Butch's relatives who could have given me the sad news. I had only his after-death dream visit as my touchstone of truth that he had passed. Later I would find out that he had died on that July day in 1990—at the precise moment he had come to me in the dream.

He was just thirty-eight years old.

My beloved Butch had indeed come to me to let me know that he loved me forever and would never be far away.

About a year after Butch's first dream visit I at last received validation of his death, when my husband and I were at a local gift shop. One of his relatives came up to me, and after we exchanged pleasantries there was a brief pause in the conversation and then he asked, "You did hear what happened to Butch, right?"

I glanced at my husband, as I had shared the dream with him. "He died, right?" I asked.

The relative looked stunned and finally stammered, "But, how did you know? There was nothing in the newspapers."

Again I glanced at my husband.

"Because he came to me in a dream and told me he was gone."

The relative just stared at me as if I had suddenly morphed into something totally unrecognizable, then he sort of said a quick goodbye and left.

And it was as simple and as complicated as that.

Butch did keep his word and returned on several other occasions.

Sometimes, he would flit through my mind as an errant thought, and then just as quickly pass from my inner vision. I sometimes wondered if, like my grandparents, I didn't really want to let go of Butch, feeling that on an emotional level any relationship with him was better than none.

I only hoped that my yearning to keep him close to me wasn't preventing him from moving forward on the other side, but then I knew that if that were so, Butch wouldn't hesitate to tell me.

As time passed I was deeply involved in my writing career, and Butch came to me in dreams to alert me to what he felt was a potentially bad situation. Sometimes he just came to let me know of his spiritual progress.

One such dream visit came about ten years ago.

It was one of those balmy afternoons in early spring, when the promise of warm days to come teases and mingles with the hint of winter past still flavoring the air.

It is not often in dreams that I see either what I am wearing or what I look like, but on this occasion I was able to see myself with great clarity.

I was in the ladies' room of a very large banquet hall and was combing my now-permed and short hair. I was wearing the pink gown that I had worn for my senior prom. All around me other girls, all appearing to be about age eighteen, were also putting on makeup, adjusting bra straps, and teasing and fixing their hair. I didn't recognize any of them and we really took no notice of one another. There was lots of giggling and laughter going on as all the girls mind-talked with one another. I smoothed my dress and exited the bathroom and moved across the sparsely populated wooden dance floor to a huge table covered with a white tablecloth. On this table was every kind of food available, from salads to pasta to rolls and desserts. It looked delicious, yet no one but me seemed interested in the food.

At the far end of the room a band was playing a song I recognized from my senior prom—the one Butch had taken me to all those years ago, or had it been only recently? Time seemed somewhat jumbled in my mind.

Seeing no one I recognized, I moved to the buffet table to partake of some of the salad—and there standing behind the table and grinning at me was Butch!

He had on the same white tuxedo jacket he had worn at my school's senior prom.

"Well, hello, gorgeous," he said with his mind. "I didn't know if you'd be able to make it or not. I didn't give up hope, though, and I waited for you."

He stepped out from behind the table and came up to me.

Still somewhat dazed by his youthful appearance and his presence, I watched as he took my hand and lifted it to his lips, kissing the palm slowly and sending a feeling of joy and warmth through me.

He held my hand in his. "Would you like to dance, babe? This song was the theme of your prom and one of your favorites, right?"

I recognized the song instantly: "Love Is Blue" by Paul Mauriat. It is a song that speaks of lost love and existing in a gray and blue world—it is a song of remorse and intense longing, and it all so perfectly fit with this moment.

Butch led me slowly out onto the now-empty dance floor. All the other couples formed a circle around us, seeming to blend into the darkness at that outer rim.

I went into Butch's arms and he drew me close to him. I could feel the solidness of his body. I lay my head on his shoulder and we began to move instinctively and easily with the smooth and natural rhythm we had always had with one another. I closed my eyes and was totally oblivious to everything but being with him and enjoying this rare and very special time together.

It was like a dream within a dream.

The violins mourned and all the instruments blended— all echoing my joyful sorrow at being in my first love's arms once again.

Sometime during our dance a golden glow of light had begun to shine down on us. I opened my eyes a bit when I felt its warmth cascading on my head and along my arms. I looked up at Butch and he smiled and kissed my forehead gently.

The song ended and he hugged me and then took my hand, lacing his fingers through mine in that old familiar way as he led me back to the now-empty table. The band and all the other people in the room vanished as if they had never existed. Everything was very quiet.

Butch put his finger under my chin and lifted my face up to his. He ever so tenderly kissed my lips just as he had done when he was alive, and then he carefully released me.

"I hope you enjoyed yourself. I did this all for you so that you could see that I'm okay and that I still love you and will always be here whenever you need me."

I whispered, my voice husky with unshed tears, "Thank you for coming. I love you too, babe."

He went to stand behind the table. He winked at me and then was gone. The room seemed to shut down after that, and I stood as the light faded and I awoke.

Butch was a remarkable spirit who gave me further proof that the soul retains every bit of the personality quirks, likes, dislikes, and methods of coping that the embodied person had on Earth. He also dispelled my stagnant thoughts that I had presumed about spirits only appearing dressed in whatever outfit they were buried or cremated in. Butch, like Grandpa and a few other spirits I was to meet, was able to change his attire to suit the surroundings of the dream. I do not know what he was dressed in when he was cremated, and it really made no difference. Casual or formal, Butch was always elegantly clad and gorgeous to my eyes, and it would be logical that his fashion sense like his personality would be intact on the other side.

And to the present date, the timeless echoes of Butch's loving and caring presence continues in my life.

In June 2011 I decided to commemorate the date of my senior prom by sending flowers to his gravesite located in California. I contacted a florist there and basically duplicated the handheld bouquet he had given me for that glorious event, with the exception of substituting two red sweetheart roses in the center of the arrangement.

By divine intervention I got in contact with a wonderful person at the cemetery who was very happy to take photos of the flowers at his gravesite and thus bridge the gap from three thousand miles away.

On the anniversary day of the prom I returned to my high school cafeteria where the prom had been held forty-two years before. As I walked toward my destination through a hall now totally silent and devoid of students or any signs of life, I felt the echoes of the past surround me. In the cafeteria I stood in the semi-darkness and closed my eyes and listened. The room still held the essence of those days, and I felt the joy and excitement of that magical night in 1969 slip into my heart and soothe me.

Back home some incredible things occurred that centered around Butch. The first was the finding of a letter from him for which I had been searching for several weeks—a letter he had written to me in June 1968. The second amazing thing was a sort of mind linkage I initiated with him during the early afternoon hours of June 20, 2011. I mentally asked him if the flowers had been delivered to his gravesite yet. The answer came back as a shout in his voice, "Not yet." Then at about twenty minutes to two in the afternoon East Coast time I again attempted a mind linkage, and Butch responded with, "They're on their way. They should be here by two." Thinking that meant two o'clock New York time I began to get very excited. Then it occurred to me to call the florist in California. The woman who answered told me that the flowers would be delivered "by two," and of course I had been wrong. It was California time, not New York time, and Butch had been exactly right about the whole thing!

To me the most moving part of this experience, much like what occurred when I placed the geranium on Beverly's grave in May, is that the dead are aware of our continuing care of their gravesites and are very thankful for the time we spend remembering them. Still, the most interesting part was the finding of the aforementioned letter from Butch, dated June 24, 1968, that I had been searching for over the previous months.

And so the synchronistic events I always associate with the possibility of a dream visit began to happen, and I knew in my heart that Butch would come to me.

That night I found myself with Butch. We were driving along a dark country road that I somehow felt was near his youthful home about an hour away. We were sitting side by side in his convertible. The convertible's top was down; the night was velvety cool and full of stars; and crickets chirped from the meadows and forests around us.

Butch pulled the car off the road and we just sat, holding hands and breathing in the joy of being alone together again.

I looked at him and saw that he was dressed in clothing that seemed to alternate between the tuxedo he had worn for the prom and the familiar yellow short-sleeved shirt and slacks. I seemed to be in my prom dress and then a white eyelet-lace short-sleeved blouse and cutoff jean shorts.

We were both in our teens.

The car radio had been playing in the background, but I couldn't make out the music. Butch turned off the ignition and silence enveloped us.

Soon I was in his arms and we were kissing and just holding onto one another.

After a few moments he mind-talked to me. "Marilou. We never got to be alone much in those days, and tonight I wanted you to have that as a gift from me."

I snuggled in his arms and relaxed against him. I wanted to cry out at the cruelty of fate that had taken him so young—cry out about the anguish of our lost relationship. As if he knew my thoughts, he kissed my forehead and hugged me tightly.

"Things happen for a reason, babe. We can't fight it all the time. Just be happy for now."

Suddenly it was as if he began to fade slightly and then come back.

"I have to go soon. I've been a long time in spirit, and I'm not allowed to stay on Earth as long as I was before."

We shared another long and tender kiss and a hug that imbued me with such strength.

"I love you, babe," he said, smiling at me with that lopsided grin. "Thank you for the flowers."

And then the scene seemed to flicker and then faded altogether.

But the visits didn't stop there.

Butch also seemed to be able to let me know that he was continuing to watch over me in other, grander ways.

It happened that a group of my friends, Dan, and I went out to a local restaurant in October of 2011. We were all eating and enjoying one another's company when I heard over the piped-in music a very familiar song. Chills wafted up my arms and my scalp prickled.

It was a song Butch and I had absolutely loved: "Incense and Peppermints" by the Strawberry Alarm Clock. I grabbed the arm of my friend who was seated next to me and told her to listen to the song being played.

"Oh, my gosh!" she exclaimed. "Butch!" Dan also recognized what was occurring.

But most interesting of all was that two of the words of the song, *children behave*, seemed to stand out to me for some reason. During those long-ago days when Butch and I were a couple, many of the grown-ups in our lives seemed overly concerned about us behaving. One of Butch's relatives in particular always admonished us every time we left her home to go for a ride in the country, to a store, or back to Butch's house. She always said, "Now you two behave!"

Dan told me that when he had gotten up to go to the salad bar, he saw that same relative enter the restaurant—just as those words, *children behave*, were playing!

There was no coincidence to this event in my mind— Butch wanted me to know that the relative was nearby.

I silently thanked him and continued to enjoy the time with Dan and my friends.

The morning of the fourth of January, 2012, was gloomy with snow spitting from a dreary sky. I was up at about six-thirty in the morning and was writing away on an article I was hoping to send to a magazine. The story was about the death of a woman's son.

Around ten in the morning I began to feel as if I hadn't slept in days, and that old familiar sensation of being dragged down to sleep overtook me. I lay down and spent several restless moments before I fell into a deep slumber.

I found myself standing in a sort of old lunchroom very much like the dining room of a once-elegant restaurant. The floors beneath my feet were made of pitted and nearly rotted wood. The scattered tables around were also rather shabby and of the long, fold-out buffet style, sans tablecloths and with stained and pitted tops.

I stood uncertainly in the center of the room while many people milled about, seeming to be unsure of where to go or what to do next.

Within what felt like seconds I sensed Butch nearby.

The thought quickly crossed my mind that it seemed absolutely incongruous for such an elegant soul to be in such a decrepit place.

I moved closer and took a look at him.

He smiled up at me wanly, as if it took every bit of his reserve energy to lift his dear mouth into that oh-so-familiar lopsided grin.

He seemed to alternate between looking okay and extremely tired and ill.

He was wearing a winter corduroy coat with toggle buttons, black slacks, and the familiar shiny dark loafers.

I went up to him and he mind-talked to me. "Hey, babe. How are you?"

I responded in the same manner that I was fine, and told him that he didn't look very good.

He stood with great effort and put his arm around me. The coat vanished, and he was now in a white button-down shirt, crisply ironed and open at the collar. The slacks and shoes stayed the same.

He drew me aside and leaned in and kissed me tenderly on the mouth. It seemed that I caught the brief scent of "ancientness" about him.

We walked through the very crowded room to a pair of stairs that were put in backwards, and I climbed to the top and came back with a notebook and some markers. We returned to sit at one of the tables, and I began to draw with a green marker. The picture was of a small Christmas tree. I told him that if he had the strength, this was something he might enjoy doing.

He shook his head and then leaned over as if he were going to be sick.

I got up from the table, took a napkin, dipped it into a glass of water, and washed his face. He looked up at me with thankful eyes.

"I love you, babe," he said with a hoarse voice.

I looked closely at his face and noticed that his cheeks were now glowing a healthy pink. I placed my hand on his face gently and then ran my hand through his hair—something he had never allowed much when we were dating—and found that it no longer was soft to my touch, but dry and lifeless.

"I love and miss you so much," I said, feeling suddenly very tired myself.

He took my hand and kissed it and maintained eye contact. "At least your love is genuine," he said, emotion making his voice unsteady.

I now noticed that his arms were stick-thin and his face had altered to something unfamiliar. He stood with great difficulty and folded me in his arms and held me very close to his painfully thin body. "I'm so tired, Marilou. I've been back and forth between here and that other place of peace and I'm exhausted. I need to rest for a while. That means I'm leaving you on your own for a bit, but don't worry. I'll keep a close watch on you and make sure you're okay."

I held him tightly, feeling the bones of his body beneath my fingers.

He continued to hold me out in his arms and looked at me. "I've got to go. Things are happening. I'll be back as soon as I can."

He kissed me on the cheek and was gone.

This dreamtime with Butch was exhausting for me on all levels. I awoke feeling very groggy and almost as if I was coming out of a long sickness. My body was shivering with emotion and my teeth were nearly chattering. I felt a deep, bone coldness course through me, and I knew, on a soul level, that Butch was gone for an indeterminate period.

I sat on the bed and considered that Butch's exhausting soul travels between dimensions resonated to another one of my dear departed friends, actor Jeremy Brett, whom we will read about in a later chapter.

I wondered if I was hurting Butch by wanting him to stay near me.

But, knowing Butch—who never did anything he didn't want to in life—I felt secure in knowing that the choice was his.

Just about three weeks after this last difficult dreamtime with Butch, he was back, peering around a corner of one of the rooms of Pleasant View—grinning at me mischievously and being his very loving and caring self. He was now seventeen again, healthy and full of playfulness. I noticed he was wearing the same outfit he had worn the day he had taken me to my high school graduation: a gold shirt with brown stripes, gray slacks, and dark loafers.

He grabbed my hand and we ran outside into the warm summer sunshine, and the delight of falling in love all over again enveloped us in a sensation of pure joy. He also left me for a moment and returned with a small blue outfit he told me he had once worn when he was a baby. When I asked if I could have it to keep, he told me, "Not yet," and I held it close and then returned it to him. He kissed me tenderly and said he would be back again soon. He vanished quickly, and I stood in the sunshine and listened to the birds singing all around me before waking up.

I know Butch will continue to be my solace and one of my very special angels for as long as he wishes. I do not want to keep him bound to Earth if that is what he does not want. Our teenage love relationship was one of compassion, fairness, trust, and deep understanding.

Butch's ever-constant love is a safe harbor I can retreat to for comfort—just as it was when he was in physical form and he and I rode those endless country roads and stopped to talk for hours, touching one another gently and holding on to the innocence of a true and precious first love that will endure for all eternity.

chapter five

A Powerful Ghost and a Writing Project

Sometime in the early 1990s my husband Dan and I took a vacation to Groton, Connecticut. From this vantage point we would be able to access Mystic Seaport as well as Misquamicut Beach in Westerly, Rhode Island.

While Dan checked us in at the front desk of the motel where we were staying, I went to peruse some local magazines, newspapers, and brochures spread out on a coffee table in the lobby. I picked up a few and took them to our room. Later I read through them, coming to a stop at an article about a castle located nearby, in Hadlyme, Connecticut. This was Gillette Castle State Park, and it had been the last earthly home of an actor/playwright/inventor named William H. Gillette (1853–1937), a man I had never heard of until I read the article that day.

As I read the article aloud to Dan, an intense feeling of longing came over me to go to the place. I told Dan, and we agreed that it would be one of our stops before heading home.

I don't think I will ever forget the incredible emotions that I felt when we turned onto the road that led to the castle. From the moment we moved through the entrance I felt a deep peace and an odd sense of déjà vu.

When we parked and walked down the winding path to the terrace and climbed the stone stairs, a sensation unlike any I had ever experienced awaited me. On the top step I paused to run my hand along the rough surface of the native stone that Gillette had used to build his castle home. Immediately an intense warmth spread up my arm, and I felt my scalp prickle as if a small charge of electricity was running a path through my body. Within seconds of this odd sensation, a male voice shouted crisply and clearly in my mind, "Welcome home!"

Dan and I went up onto the terrace and stood to look out over the magnificent view of the Connecticut River.

Then we bought tickets and went inside. While there I told Dan about my experience.

Walking the expanse of the castle I continued to feel that overwhelming sensation of being *home again*.

And I knew things.

Things about the castle about which I really had no pre-knowledge.

For example, I knew that the carpet on the main floor was somehow "wrong" and that in the upstairs office the carpet beneath the laid-over rug was the right one, or close to it. I also wondered why the water fountain over the massive stone fireplace wasn't working.

There came over me an incredible and intense yearning to immediately know more about the man who had dreamed up this unique and beautiful edifice, who had supervised every aspect of its construction, and who had lived in it until he was taken ill and died in a hospital in Hartford in April 1937. Thankfully, several of the seasonal workers were very willing to share information with me. The overseer of the castle and his wife were also amazing resources. In fact, these two would take Dan and me, and a psychic medium, on a moonlit night tour of the castle, when the spirit of Mr. Gillette seemed to be lingering just on the other side of the darkness in the upstairs rooms.

Having had some small success as a writer of nonfiction articles, I asked the Gillette Castle overseer if there was a biography written about the man and was told that there had been "something" done in the 1970s but it was not an officially published book. It was available at the library just up the road from the castle. After leaving the castle, which was actually named "Seventh Sister" by Gillette because of the mountain it was situated on, Dan and I went to the library and the librarian ran off a copy of the book for me.

William Gillette, his occupation as an actor/playwright, the times in which he had lived, and his castle home held an allure for me beyond comprehension. And so it was that my husband and I were to return many times during those early years as the biography I wanted so deeply to write took form and shape in my heart and mind.

Eventually I was allowed access and free run of the castle during the pre-opening early hours and given the rare and wonderful privilege of being allowed to go up to the tower room to begin my early writing of the life story of the owner/builder. This privilege was rare indeed, as the public was not allowed access to this portion of the place.

I was also allowed to sit in his bedroom on his bed and write. From this vantage point I could look over the balcony and see the great room below all the way to the lush green leaves of the plants in the conservatory. I usually closed my eyes and mentally tried to cast myself back to the time when Mr. Gillette would have called this place his home. I watched the images in my mind come and go. I saw his favorite tabby cats run through the halls to greet him. I heard the singsong voices of his two Japanese servants chatting about the dinner menu. I inhaled the aroma of summer breezes and the scent of the river that pushed through the open windows. Gradually the flurry of activity created by the summer tour guides faded, and I entered a new reality where I felt the years slip backwards as I became one with William Gillette and Seventh Sister.

I wandered into his closet, and the aroma of cherry pipe tobacco followed me in and out like a wafting spirit.

I sensed his presence very nearby and had the uncanny feeling that he was watching me. My body would feel cold and occasional gooseflesh would rise up on my arms.

I knew William was assessing me.

I allowed it because I so much wanted to merge with his world and be accepted by him.

When the castle opened for tours, I left the bedroom and went up to the tower room. Here were incredible vistas to survey on all points. The roadway from the parking lot was visible from one window. On another side was the roof where William had kept a garden and beyond that the river and the far shore.

Several times when I was in the tower room and deeply absorbed in my writing, I saw a quick shadow figure flit past my peripheral vision. It seemed to rush up the stairway, fly straight through the wall to the outside, and fly back in. I quietly acknowledged the spirit and continued writing and playing my cassette of Chopin—one of Mr. Gillette's favorite composers.

In the process of writing, I also began interviewing people who had actually known William Gillette. One of these dear people made sure that I would record her age as "one hundred and one and a half"! The memories came easily to those who had been in the presence of this great man.

Then I began a new job at a local clinic and there met a woman whose coming had been foretold to me by a psychic I had called about a year prior. As soon as she heard about my project she became somewhat alarmed and told me in no uncertain terms to "be very careful" because, as she saw it, "he [William Gillette] is a very powerful spirit." Her warnings were to become truthful in the near future when Mr. Gillette decided that it was his turn to come to me in dreams. And not just a mere dream of a historical figure or one of those everyday dreams that most people have about meeting an important person from another time, but a visit from William Gillette in my dreams that allowed him to give me his own personal take on the book I was writing about his life.

It was a compelling, incredible experience from one of the stage's most powerful men.

I truly do believe that every biographer must, on some level, fall either half or totally in love with his or her subject. I have always reasoned that if there is no love for the person being written about, then there is no passion on the page. Falling in love with William Gillette was easy for me.

He had, at an early age, known both loss and illness and these would be a continual theme in his life. He attained fame and fortune as an actor/playwright during a period in history that has always felt like *home* to me. He enjoyed the company of many of the greats of the literary and theatrical worlds. Having been a neighbor of Mark Twain, Harriet Beecher Stowe, and other notables, he was a source of great fascination to me, and as I delved deeper into his psyche I felt a kinship and a soul connection that made it seem as if he and I had known one another for a very, very long time. In fact, in later years I would find that we shared a genealogical attachment, however distant, through my father's side of the family that connected William and me through marriage.

William, or Will, as he was known to his close friends and family members, was a man of many moods. He habitually turned away reporters—sometimes after having a bit of verbal sport with them—and thus rarely granted interviews. He both detested and distrusted biographers and had no liking for non-professionalism on the stage. For the most part he did as his manager, Charles Frohman, instructed and remained aloof from the public, assuring that the persona and illusion he created as an actor stayed intact. In the late 1800s he would write (with the blessing of Sir Arthur Conan Doyle) the play version of Doyle's *Sherlock Holmes*, bringing the fictitious detective alive for audiences over 1,300 times during William's lifetime.

A man of contrasts, he could be both sarcastic and caring. He adored cats, children, and inventing. His kindness and generosity were enjoyed by many, and he most often preferred to be an anonymous donor to a cause that would help someone less fortunate.

In his will he hinted at being cognizant in the afterlife of the fate of his castle home. He had also, I found, dabbled a bit in spiritualism himself.

So, in essence, for me the stage was set to begin an incredible relationship with a man who, at the time I began working on his biography, had not only been dead for almost sixty years, but who also had been buried on my birthday date in 1937.

I was in the beginning stages of assembling the massive material required to work on the biography. It was a daunting task, as Mr. Gillette had, I found, destroyed a great many of his own personal letters just prior to his death. His other letters, play material, photos, and so forth were in many collections both private and organizational. The landscape of his eighty-plus years of earthly life stretched from California to Europe back to New York and Connecticut and everywhere in between.

I had also begun to search for a publisher and had found one in the person of Mr. Jack Tracy at Gaslight Publications, Inc. I did a cold call to Jack—something not typically done, but when Jack heard of my enthusiasm for the project he quickly became a mentor and a lifeline during those early years, supplying me with contacts and mailing me information he deemed helpful. He was overjoyed with my outline for the book and did all he could to encourage me to completion. Jack always felt that I was the only one who could write

William Gillette's biography and his faith in me was tremendous and inspiring.

So it was that in the autumn of 1993, Mr. Gillette decided it was time to make his first contact with me in a dream—and a very memorable meeting it was.

In the dream I found myself outside the castle conservatory. It was a summer day, sunny with pleasant temperatures. Over the stone wall I could see the Connecticut River stretching out, and many boats were going up and down at a leisurely pace.

I had the great sense that I was waiting for someone, and so I stood and enjoyed the view.

Suddenly, the sensation that someone was coming and the aroma of cherry pipe tobacco filled the air.

I turned to my left and there was Mr. Gillette! He walked straight out of the wall of the conservatory and stood in front of me. His blue eyes were alight with intense interest and also burning with a touch of angry inquisitiveness. He wore a robe of deep maroon with gold embroidery tied at the waist. A dark cravat with an opal stick pin was at his throat. He was tall and thin with dark wavy hair, and he seemed to tower over me. I would say that his age was about forty, even though I knew he had been eighty-three when he had passed.

Though his presence was overwhelming, I did not flinch from him or betray any unease, as I sensed he would see this as a sign of weakness.

He spoke in my mind. "So. You want to write my biography?"

"Yes. Very much" I responded mentally.

"You'll need my permission to do that, you know."

"I know."

"Well, I'll give it, but there are going to be ground rules."

"I understand."

"It will be factual to the utmost. It will show me in a good light. No straying off on tangents. No conjectures or assumptions. In the beginning you will not work on the thing at night. When I find I approve of it you may commence night writing."

I was about to question him as to the reason why I could not write the book at night when he leaned down to me and looked me in the eyes.

"Do we have an understanding?"

"Yes." I responded, my gaze not wavering from the intense glare of his steely deep blue eyes.

I swallowed my questions and kept my attention on him.

"Good. Now I have to leave for a while. But first I must give you something."

I thought he was going to give me access to a secret hiding place where I might find some important letters that had escaped the prying of others.

Instead—

I watched in fascination as a round, wavering ball of light shot out of his solar plexus and into mine.

The event was totally unexpected, and I felt the light pass through me as a sort of warm connection between him and me that somehow solidified our mental ground rules connecting us on a level that would forevermore be beyond soul deep.

After this I had the most overwhelming urge to hug him. I stepped closer.

He instantly held up his hand. "No! You cannot touch me! I am totally in spirit and have been for a long time. The contact could harm you."

"I'm sorry," I muttered.

"There is no need to apologize. You must be careful of those in spirit who invite you to touch them. Some may know their limitations. Others may mean you harm." He paused. "I like you, Marilou, and would not wish to harm you ever."

"Thank you." I muttered.

"Now, we both have a great deal of work to do, you on your end and me on mine. I'll be back soon to gauge your progress."

As I watched, he walked back to the wall of the conservatory and stepped through it and back into the castle.

Shortly after this dream encounter, my publisher began to tell me stories about some who had attempted to write the biography of William Gillette and had suffered from some unusual experiences. Jack wasn't really a believer in any of the coincidences, but he was apparently concerned enough to share the details with me as a way of caution.

This talk bothered me on many levels, and I decided to keep my dream experience with Mr. Gillette a secret.

Then, in July 1994, I was inspired to have a tea at the castle to honor the one hundred and forty-first year of Mr. Gillette's birth.

It was a grand event. Many, myself included, dressed in period costume. I gave a speech gleaned from my interviews with those who had known him. Several of those marvelous people were present. I read letters from many notables, including Mary Ellis, the actress who, in her nineties, had recently appeared in the Granada Television production of *Sherlock Holmes* starring British actor Jeremy Brett. Mr. Brett and I were already having a marvelous trans-Atlantic relationship of mutual love and support.

During the tea, one of the guests was injured. A young man fell, and one of the guests told me he had broken his wrist.

Many whispered that Mr. Gillette was somehow responsible.

I kept silent, and because of my talk with Jack Tracy I secretly wondered if they were right.

And I also began to wonder if my workmate had been correct about the power of this spirit to cross the threshold between life and death and influence outcomes.

The years passed and for reasons both personal and professional the biography was stored away as I began working on other projects, continuing to work at an office near my home.

One day I decided that it was time to restart the biography, and so I made a phone call to Jack Tracy at the home number he had given to me. A message from the operator said the number had been disconnected.

Odd.

Then I looked up the listing in *The Writer's Market,* and his publishing company was not listed any longer, but it was there as a part of another publishing house. I called them and found out to my horror that Jack had died a "few years ago."

I don't remember what words I mumbled to the man I spoke to.

Jack had been the one to both warn and encourage me with this project. I was disheartened to know that all the work and energy and care he had put into the project and his absolute faith in me as a writer was somehow lost.

I even waited for Jack to come to me in a dream and tell me how to proceed, but he never did.

I would have given up then, but I knew in my heart that this book was worthwhile and that it would serve a larger purpose if I were to complete the work, so I called the second publisher back a few days later and followed up with a letter. They said that they would definitely be interested in seeing the manuscript and to send along the entire thing to them when it was complete.

I don't know why, but I felt Jack pulling some strings for me from the other side of life's doorway.

Shortly after this, Mr. Gillette paid me another dream visit. It was about a month after finding out about Jack. I was again deeply asleep and found myself in the castle, this time seated on a large sofa in front of the lit fireplace. It was evening, and the room danced with shadows as the fire in the huge fireplace spit and the logs cracked and snapped.

I felt again that I was waiting for someone.

Soon, a lanky shadow detached itself from the deeper darkness near the terrace doors and came toward me with a tea tray in its hands.

It was Mr. Gillette.

He set the tray down on a table before me and began to mind-talk as he poured out cups of steaming tea.

"Hello again, Marilou. I assume you drink tea?"

I nodded yes, and without any further questions he began to add cream and two teaspoons of sugar to the cup, stirred it, and handed it to me.

It was exactly the way that I took my tea and though I was entranced at how he knew this, I decided to let it go unmentioned.

He sat down beside me.

I sipped my tea and found it to be very good and quite bracing, exactly what I needed. I asked him with my mind, "Don't you drink tea, Mr. Gillette?"

"No," he smiled across at me. "Food and drink are indulgences for the living. We in spirit no longer require sustenance of any sort."

I continued to sip my tea.

He settled against the sofa and laid his arm along the back of it. He was wearing the same robe as he had before. The opal stick pin in his cravat twinkled in the light of the fire.

"Are you quite ready to continue with the project now?" he asked matter-of-factly.

"Yes," I replied.

"Good. I'm pleased with it. You may begin writing at night now if you wish."

"Thank you," I said.

We sat in silence for a while watching the fire.

"I'll take my leave of you then. Call on me when you need me and remember my ground rules about the book."

"I will. Thank you."

Without any further ado he simply stood and walked off into the darkness, and I awoke knowing that he and I had solidified our negotiations about the biography.

Shortly after this, my dear Butch came to me in a dream. He seemed extremely concerned.

We were in a place I did not recognize—something like a large room where events take place. He mind-spoke to me, "Be careful, babe. That man you are writing about is powerful in many ways."

"I promise I'll be careful," I said.

Butch then vanished quickly.

About a month later Will again came to me in a dream, and this time his demeanor was more alluring.

We were once more seated before the fireplace in the castle, and I sensed it was near dawn, as a vague rosy pale light was streaming in through the windows.

He sat down beside me on the sofa.

There was also an unfathomable ethereal quality about the dream—as if it had altered from being a mere dream and had somehow become a time portal I might be able to choose to slip through and into if I wished. Of course, the lure of the Victorian times has always held an intense fascination for me—and it was as though my host knew that, and, much like my childhood near-death-experience guide, Emmie, who had tried to get me to cross over to the sunlit meadow to stay with her, William Gillette seemed to want me in his time.

"You like it here, don't you? Would you like to stay?" he asked, his eyes deep blue and very serious as they gazed deeply into mine.

I looked around.

"It is very tempting, but no, thank you. I'm fine where I am," I replied.

"Don't make a decision you'll regret."

"I'm not. I have a husband and family and friends, a job and pets in my time, and I don't want to leave them."

"Suit yourself," he said, and then simply vanished.

I awoke a few moments later, quickly and with my heart pounding in my chest. The flavor of this dream visit lingered for several days, and when I told my friend at work about it, she again cautioned me to be careful.

Yet another lesson about the dead then became apparent. Some were quite content to come to me and visit and only allow our worlds to mingle with boundaries intact. William's visit taught me to be cognizant of the fact that my longings for escape and life in another time could prove to be my undoing. I would now learn to be more vigilant and not to allow those longings to be so evident to spirits. It could, I knew, prove fatal.

There were many other incidents with Mr. Gillette throughout my days of revising the earlier portions of the biography.

One day my husband and I traveled to Farmington, Connecticut, to the cemetery where Will and his family were buried. We had no guide to help us and walked around the old section until Dan found the graves.

I brought white roses for Will, and when I bent down to lay the one on his grave his crisp, clear voice shouted in my mind: "What are you doing here?"

I mind-told him that I was bringing flowers for the graves.

Again came the mental command, "Thank you. Now please leave. You shouldn't be here. This is no place for you!"

I never knew if he was warning me of some unseen forces or just being Will, but after taking a photo of his grave with the flower on it, we left.

Quite a few years later I would find that this cemetery was extremely active with orbs, ghostly mists, and spirit voices.

Perhaps, I reasoned, Will was attempting to protect me from those of his ilk who wouldn't be as concerned about my safety as he now was.

Will still echoes around my life as I work on the biography—sometimes helpful, sometimes exasperating, especially when I find I need just another few letters or photos to complete a particular section of the book.

He still comes to me in dreams, usually taking me back to the castle and leading me up a flight of stairs to a tower room unlike any I saw when I was there. This room is like a loft full of dust and plush red velvet chairs and sofas and bookcases full of books whose bindings are worn and whose covers are battered. There is a desk there and a few candles in holders scattered about, the white wax dripped long ago into huge chunks around the bases. Here is age and near-decay, solitude, and unnerving, lingering memories. It is not at all an uncomfortable room, just eerie and lonely, and timelessness hangs heavy in the air.

Of late, Will has also come to me in my dreams and begun to take me to another large cathedral-like building where oak-carved stairways disappear into far-off darkness and many classes seem to be going on. There is an echoing tone to this huge building, and I have the feeling that, like Grandpa's transformation place, this building exists outside of time and space and is not a part of any earthly dimension.

Still, as long as I walk behind or next to my guiding spirit Will, I feel safe and protected.

And he would never, in any of his visits to me, offer an explanation as to why I was, at first, not allowed to work on the biography in the evening hours. I never asked him. I trusted his wisdom about such things and let it go.

All in all, it seems now that William Gillette and I have come to find peace with one another, and I hope that the project will soon be completed and that he will be very pleased with the result.

Of all the things I've learned during the writing of this biography, the most important one is that the mortality of man encompasses all. For me the people who inhabited William Gillette's world—Samuel Clemens (Mark Twain), Harriet Beecher Stowe, Rev. Joseph H. Twichell, among others, and all of Will's family and friends—they have all become very, very real to me. As time passed I felt as though I had actually known them personally. And this is as it should be. Their joys and sorrows and triumphs and tragedies have become mine as my world and theirs have steadily become entwined over the years. I rejoice when I read of a birth or wedding or anniversary party. I mourn when I read of a beloved friend or family member dying. I *miss* the departed one and feel the anguish of loss just as keenly as the mourners themselves do.

Also as enlivening to me is the essence of the time and place that mark the lives of these dear ones. Hartford, Connecticut, in the nineteenth and early twentieth centuries seems my home. I wander in a state of dreamtime and enjoy the aromas of newly blossoming fruit trees and feel uplifted by the sun's warmth as spring and summer meld into one another. I hear in my mind the wafting notes of Susan Warner's piano playing drifting out over the lawns and glades of the little community known as Nook Farm, where these literary and important people of the time lived out their days. Croquet on the lawn next to Mark Twain's unusual and unique home. The swish of long skirts, the murmur of voices on those long-ago summer nights speak to my soul of home and family and community and heart.

The same yearning that filled my heart as a child—the yearning that I felt at Pleasant View then and now—comes and rises up in my mind and transports me back to those "gilded" days of joy.

As each chapter of the book takes shape and form, I find I move like a wraith through their days and make them my own.

Writing a biography of someone else's life from long ago truly does make you aware of your own mortality.

Every one of the personages who move through the pages of my book on William Gillette's life are gone now. Some are dead well over a hundred years—even though to me this still seems impossible.

But then, immersing oneself in another time and place eradicates all of the old familiar lines of judgment. All dimensions blur, and what once was now seems real. By the same token, what is real now seems blurred and out of focus.

This is what comes from descending fully into the life of a biographical subject.

And this is, no doubt, exactly what William Gillette was attempting to communicate to me when he came to me in my dreams, admonished me about the particulars of the book, and later tried to coerce me into coming into his world and living in his time. An impossibility, to be sure, but then I think a biography is, in truth, a time machine—and as a writer he knew that about himself and then awakened it in me. If any writing creation—be it book, play, or poem—gives the reader a sense of time and place, if it transports and eradicates the lines between then and now and causes the reader to feel as if they actually know the people in that other place, then the creation, to my mind, has done its job.

And as an update to William's continued presence in my life I offer the following two recent experiences.

On June 14, 2011, my husband and I traveled to Hartford, so that I could take part in an event honoring author Harriet Beecher Stowe and the two-hundredth anniversary of her birth. Selected persons were to read ten-minute segments from her landmark anti-slavery book, *Uncle Tom's Cabin*. The event took place in the home that sits across from Harriet's house. When it was my turn to step up the podium and just prior to my reading, the aroma most affiliated with William—cherry pipe tobacco—drifted behind me. I turned slightly, almost expecting his tall, thin frame to be standing there watching me. Just seconds before I began to read I heard his voice in my mind: "Go on, now! You'll do fine."

I acknowledged his encouraging presence silently and began to read.

In the car on the way home after the event again came the aroma of the cherry pipe tobacco, and this time Dan smelled it as well. It hung in the air inside the car and then vanished as soon as we both acknowledged William's presence and after I thanked him for his kindness and protection on the journey homeward.

His guidance and great protective energy are an incredible comfort to me as I continue to reassemble the story of his life.

chapter six

A Friendship That Transcends Death

Since earliest childhood I have been fascinated with Sir Arthur Conan Doyle's great detective, Sherlock Holmes. By the time I was seven or eight, Grandpa was buying me a book a week, and when he came home one winter's afternoon with Doyle's Sherlock Holmes story "The Adventure of the Speckled Band," I promptly went to sit on my little red chair in front of the open oven door of the old kitchen woodstove and read the entire thing through that day and into the night. Later on, I read it aloud to my grandparents, who were also riveted by the tale. After this, Grandpa purchased all of the Holmes books for me one by one until I had a complete library.

They were books I cherished and re-read over and over again until the pages became semi-tattered and stained with my childish fingerprints.

The allure of that fictional detective who was intuitive to a fault, and who cut through all the artifice to the real clues of the crime, seized me in a powerful grip and I was captivated with the prowess of Sherlock and his uncanny charm.

As usually happens, life intervened and the things of childhood were put aside so that the pursuits of school and work could take center stage. Yet, despite this, my hero worship of the great detective never ceased or lost its fervor. Sometimes an old black-and-white movie of Holmes starring Basil Rathbone would be on the television, and I would take the time to watch closely, indulging myself in the mental game of trying to outwit Holmes and find the clues before he did.

Sometimes I wished that I could go back in time to those fog-shrouded London streets of Sherlock's day and follow along beside him like Dr. Watson did and be an observer or a helpmate as he put the pieces of the crime together and solved the whole thing logically and smoothly.

Little wonder then that when, in the late 1980s, Dan and I found a public television broadcast of *Sherlock Holmes* starring British actor Jeremy Brett, I was again riveted. This time, though, there was something a bit different about the whole thing—I was as compelled to meet or get to know this actor, Jeremy Brett, as I would later be to write the life story of William Gillette.

I started to read some biographical information about Jeremy and found that he had been born Peter Jeremy William Huggins on November 3, 1933, in Berkswell Grange, in the West Midlands region of England. His parents were Henry William Huggins, a military colonel, and his mother was Elizabeth Cadbury Huggins, a descendent of the famous

Cadbury candy line. He had three brothers. Much like William Gillette, he had bucked the family system by aspiring to be an actor. In fact, there were several similarities between William and Jeremy. Like William, Jeremy was born into a life of relative wealth. His father, like William's, frowned upon his son becoming an actor and forbade young Peter from using the Huggins name if he entered that so-despicable field of employment, so Jeremy improvised and chose to use one of his middle names and the name *Brett* from a suit jacket label of Brett & Co.

The most memorable role I ever saw him in prior to his portrayal of Sherlock Holmes was as Freddy Eynsford-Hill, Audrey Hepburn's suitor in the movie version of *My Fair Lady*. Jeremy was the incredibly handsome young man who sang "On the Street Where You Live," and even though I later found out his voice was dubbed, it didn't matter—he was still a most handsome and captivating man to me and to so many, as well as an extremely versatile and talented actor.

Looking back from the vantage point of almost twenty years, it makes perfect sense that the two most important men in my world of writing and television friendship both portrayed my dear Sherlock Holmes—one at the beginning of the spectrum of bringing the character to life and the other who would be dubbed "the quintessential Holmes" by a new generation captivated by his on-camera presence.

In any event, it proved to be destined, and easily so, for me to get in touch with Jeremy and for him to reciprocate back.

At the time I was operating a family-based daycare and had four children in attendance. One day I decided to watch a video of Jeremy as Sherlock Holmes while the children were napping. The oldest boy in my care came in from his nap and happened to catch the tail end of one of the programs, in which Jeremy looks into the camera and has with him one of those mechanical monkeys that clap together two cymbals.

The child was totally engaged in watching. He asked me the name of the man on the television and I told him it was Mr. Brett.

Almost instantly the boy, then age about four, thought that it would be a great idea if we were to send Mr. Brett a card or a letter. The next day we did one better. We made a beautiful card and also recorded a cassette tape of us telling him about our day. I contacted the studio in London where he worked and we sent the package out.

About four months later a postcard from Jeremy arrived in the mail! He was busy filming and thanked all of us. We were thrilled!

As the rest of the year progressed, we sent cassette tapes full of songs and loving messages, little gifts, letters and cards, birthday wishes, and holiday cards. By now we had a contact outside of London to send the packages to—at a favorite restaurant of Jeremy's located at Battersea Rise. The owners saw him constantly, and they were able to deliver anything we sent to Jeremy when he stopped in. They even made a mailbox for him at the place where all the mail we sent was placed for him to pick up.

The next year in March, the phone rang at Pleasant View at 8:10 in the morning. It was Jeremy! He wanted so much to talk to the children, but they had not yet arrived. So he and I spent a half-hour chatting about every topic we could. The flow of conversation between us was eerily easy, as if we were simply picking up on things after an absence from one another of a few weeks. All too soon he had to "ring off" and go back to the set. He promised to call later in the day to talk to any of the children available.

He did as he promised and called back in the afternoon around three. One of the boys got to talk to him about his favorite television show, *Teenage Mutant Ninja Turtles*, and through the receiver I could hear Jeremy laughing and loving talking about such things. And though one of the girls was only an infant in the walker, Jeremy asked to have the phone held to her ear so that he could say hello. The girl chortled and laughed at his voice and definitely enjoyed being able to be a "big girl" almost holding on to the phone.

For the next three years the children in the daycare and I kept in constant contact with Jeremy, as he did with us. His private phone calls to me were full of encouragement for my writing career. He knew about the biography of William Gillette and urged me to complete it. He offered to do a foreword for it but said it would have to go through his agent and that they would need to see the completed manuscript. I was elated!

I was writing about the life of one of the first actors to portray Sherlock Holmes and was also now transatlantic friends with the currently popular Sherlock Holmes!

The life path I was on was becoming clearer.

Time passed, and there were often lapses in the communications between Jeremy, myself, and the children. Once, when there was an extremely long silence I called the restaurant and spoke to one of the owners who informed me that Jeremy was at a place where he could "rest." I knew Jeremy's history of depression and the heart ailment that had plagued

him since youth, so I understood and sent prayers and healing thoughts his way.

The children and I continued to send him cards and cassette tapes full of conversations and songs. One day he sent
a note with a watercolor drawing of his home in Clapham
Common and circled the portion of the building where he
lived. When my next birthday came around he called and
sang to me a portion of "On the Street Where You Live."
That dear voice, a bit older yet with those delightful British
tones singing to me a song I had loved since I first heard it
years before, made tears well up in my eyes with gratitude
for having such a dear friend.

After one of Jeremy's bouts at the "rest" site, an overwhelming feeling came over me to call him at the restaurant. I
had no idea why I was having this intense urge, and I certainly
had no way of actually knowing that he had been released or
that he would be at the place. I was going on pure institution
and followed it.

The moment I called, one of the owners exclaimed,
"Oh my goodness! How did you know, Marilou? He just
walked in!"

The phone was handed to Jeremy, and I told him about
my feeling that he would be there and that I listened to my
intuition to call him.

He was very accepting of my following my feelings and
was so glad to hear my voice. Then he said something I shall
never forget. "Marilou! How wonderful to hear your voice! I
knew you'd ring today! Thank you for caring."

After the call ended, I heard again and again in my mind
his cultured British voice saying, "I knew you'd ring today."

How had he known I would call?

How had I known that at that precise moment he would walk into the restaurant?

The connection between us, though deep from the start, was now on an even more intense level. We were, I felt, not only soul partners who understood and appreciated one another from the heart, but we also could somehow key into the whereabouts of the other through some sort of mental telepathy that had to do with trusting one's intuition.

Also, later that same day as evening drew in tight around Pleasant View, I had an incredibly strange feeling come over me and I knew in my heart that Jeremy and I would never meet in the flesh. It was a certainty that caused me grief, but I clung to the scant hope that I was wrong.

After this remarkable bonding between Jeremy and me, there followed a terrible, deep silence.

The silence stretched into an unfathomable time, and soon the stillness from him was as dark and as vast as the ocean that separated us.

I knew on a very deep level that Jeremy was very ill and somehow slipping away from me.

A sensation of overwhelming dread and helplessness overtook me.

Then, in the early morning hours of September 12, 1995, after a particularly restless night, I fell at last into a deep sleep and began to dream.

It was a gorgeous summer day. I was standing alone on a loading platform at a former worksite—but things were not exactly as I remembered them from my days of being employed at the place. It had now altered into a train station. Where the parking lot had once been train tracks stretched off down the hill and curved around behind the building.

Hundreds of people crowded around—dressed in attire from many time periods, they also represented many races. The atmosphere was one of anticipation.

Unsure of what to expect, I stayed put.

Soon was heard the sound of an approaching steam engine. Gradually the train slowed and came to a stop.

The crowd surged forward, aiming toward a particular passenger car.

The sun glinted in my eyes and I shaded them so as to see better, but all that was visible was a tall man dressed in black who was standing uncertainly on the steps of one of the passenger cars.

I stepped down from the loading dock and stood back a ways, observing the people. I could no longer see the tall man, but nearby a whole group of individuals were surrounding someone. Whoever this person was, everyone seemed very happy to see him.

I turned to leave.

Suddenly before me was a tall, slim man with dark hair and piercing deep blue eyes. He appeared to be about thirty or thirty-five years of age. When he touched me I felt an incredible golden warmth spread through my entire body and soul—I can only describe it as falling ever so deeply in love and feeling the cocoon of that perfect joy and peace fill up every fiber of the being.

I looked up into the man's face and realized it was Jeremy!

He mind-spoke to me, "I can't wait until I see you in my country."

The crowd anxiously surged around us. They wanted him for their own, and I knew I didn't really belong there.

Jeremy told me he loved me and that he would return soon.

As he was led off by the people and vanished from my sight, I stood still, knowing that he was no longer on the earthly plane—and more importantly, knowing that he and I were to be eternal friends. The meeting that had been denied us on Earth had been granted by Heaven.

That afternoon at the office a co-worker asked me if I had heard the news—Jeremy had died in his sleep of heart failure that morning. He was just sixty-one years old.

Overcome with grief I told my boss I was leaving for the day. I ran out of the office and went home in tears, my anguish cutting deep.

As with Grandpa's passing, and despite Jeremy coming to me in my dreams a few hours earlier, I felt lost, abandoned, and so totally alone.

The kind, dear man who had been my *anam cara*—which in the Irish language translates to "soul friend"—was gone. There would be no more long and deep phone conversations with him about life, my writing hopes, and his next film project. No more jokes about eating too much pasta (he said it made him "fat"), no more sympathetic murmurs from him about the tragedy of my youthful abandonment or job woes. He would never again call me "darling" or tell me he loved me by saying, "I'm reaching across the Atlantic to give you a hug."

He had been my anchor and now he was gone.

Or was he?

An odd occurrence began about a week after Jeremy's passing: every morning at precisely 8:10 a.m. the phone would ring three times and stop.

When I did answer there was only static.

I yelled hello several times into the receiver and, getting no reply, I hung up.

The second week of this, I finally understood.

I picked up the receiver, and calmly and quietly said, "Hello, Jeremy. Thank you for calling. Everything's okay here."

The calls at 8:10 in the morning came no more.

It might be said that I rely on the dead to keep their promises to return to me to let me know not only how they are faring in their new realm, but also to offer comfort and hope.

Like Grandpa, Jeremy was a man of his word.

A few weeks after the phone calls ceased, I was standing in my bedroom looking out at the early November landscape of skeletal tree branches and browned lawn covered with decaying leaves. It would have been Jeremy's sixty-second birthday, and I was thinking of the times during the past few years when the daycare children and I had sent him gifts and flowers for this day. There had been phone calls and singing and joy to share for being friends for another year.

I missed him so deeply, and I began to cry.

The air around me grew cool and seemed to hum with a soothing rhythm and energy.

Quickly an aroma of cigarette smoke, then the fragrance of a fine, rich cologne, surrounded me—the same cologne scent I had smelled wafting up to me from one of the cards Jeremy had sent to the daycare and me.

There was a very slight feeling of a deeper coldness and then the sensation of a hand resting lightly on my left shoulder. The scent of the cologne intensified.

I didn't move, but basked in the joy of Jeremy's return.

Without hesitation I spoke to him in my mind and said, "Thank you, darling, for coming to me. I'll be okay."

The scents now associated with Jeremy faded, and the temperature in the room returned to normal.

The next time Jeremy and I met in dreamtime was when he had been in spirit for about six months.

The meeting took place in a very large library.

Dressed in the attire of Sherlock Holmes and not youthened, he wore the familiar dark suit and crisp white shirt with black tie. He beckoned me by crooking his index finger, indicating that I was to follow him to a particular bookshelf.

He pointed to a book I had heard of but never read: *The Prophet*, by Kahlil Gibran. Mentally he told me to go to my local library, take the book out, and "turn to the page that begins: 'And when you crush an apple ...' and memorize it," so that I would know exactly how he felt about me.

I got the book the next day and took it home. I easily found the stanza Jeremy had told me to read. I read it over and over and truly began to comprehend the deep soul connection we had forged on Earth—a bond that even death could not break.

Here is the part that Jeremy wanted me to memorize:

"And when you crush an apple with your teeth, say to it in your heart:

'Your seeds shall live in my body,

And the buds of your tomorrow shall blossom in my heart,

And your fragrance shall be my breath,

And together we shall rejoice through all the seasons.'"

Over the brief time that our friendship grew during his earthly life, I was able to share with Jeremy, via our phone conversations, a great deal of my sadness and anger about my infancy abandonment issues. He had always done his best to calm me and to make me realize that these problems were part of the past and that no emotions on my part could affect a change. What was done was done. He was sorry for the negative parts of life I'd had; he was very grateful to my grandparents whom he said I was a "great credit to"; and he was firm in the belief that I had grown up with the family I was meant to have.

Under his careful guidance and tutelage, I came to understanding and eventually to forgiveness. I knew he was right. Each one of us was perfectly placed in the grand scheme of things, and even if we didn't see it that way, it was true.

His philosophy was sound and I accepted it.

So it was that I next embarked on a journey of self-discovery and inner concentration.

I sought out a local counselor and began sessions with him, so that I could, I hoped, at last begin to uncover the fears that had pervaded my entire life—the main one of which was the fear of abandonment that had been a part of my life since I was an infant.

The sessions proved helpful, and each week I came away with clarity of vision and a realization that Jeremy had been so right.

It wasn't surprising then that shortly after I began this therapy he came to me in a dream.

The scene of the dream was, I divined, somewhere in Cornwall, England.

It was a gorgeous sunny day in spring, and I was seated on a portion of a rocky outcropping just relaxing in the sunshine. All around were fields and rocks and many birds.

Suddenly there was the purr of a car motoring along a dirt road that led up to where I was. I shaded my eyes and saw what I believe was a tan Mercedes-Benz maneuvering along the roadway. It came to a stop and a tall, dark-haired man of about thirty got out. He was wearing a tan suit that almost matched the car. As he approached I stood up and went toward him.

"Hello, Marilou!" He called out to me with his mind. "I thought I'd find you here."

It was Jeremy, and he looked so healthy and so youthful and at peace.

"Come," he said, going ahead of me and back to the rock where I had been sitting. "Let's relax for a while and talk. I don't have much time. I have to go back very soon."

I followed and we sat side by side in the sun, listening to the cries of the birds and the soothing buzz of bees in the flowers nearby.

"Are you happy?" I asked. "Have you found your wife yet?" (His second wife, Joan Wilson, died in 1985 of cancer, and he was devastated by her loss and had gone into a serious mental decline.)

He leaned back and stretched his legs out in front of him, turning his face up to the sun as if attempting to pull its healing rays into his soul.

"No. I haven't found Joan yet, but I'm hopeful."

A few moments of silence.

"What's Heaven like?" I asked.

"Peaceful," he responded then, hesitated, and said, "Quite nice, actually."

He sat up straighter and seemed to be listening to something that was far beyond my hearing.

"Time for me to go now, but I'll be near if you need me."

He stood up, brushed off his pants, and began to walk down the hill toward his car. I got up and followed, feeling very sad that he was leaving me yet again.

He got in the car, started the engine, and rolled the window down. I had so wanted to hug him goodbye.

I started to cry.

He smiled at me. "Now. Now. None of that. I'll be around whenever you need me."

I wiped my eyes.

He put his hand out of the car window.

"Come here, Marilou."

I went up to the car door. He took my hand in his. It felt warm and real and pulsated with an energy that coursed through me like quicksilver.

"Always remember I love you very much," he said.

I clung to his hand for a few minutes and then he let go.

He drove up the road a ways and turned and came back past me. He did not look at me but kept his gaze straight ahead.

I stood and watched as the car drove into a golden pool of brilliant light and vanished.

I woke up and knew, as before, that like all those other beloved ones who had passed on, that Jeremy would never really be far away.

Our love, like the love between me and Grandpa, Grandma, and Butch, would endure for all eternity and beyond.

By September of 2010 Jeremy had been in spirit for fifteen years. I had, since that last dream visit, only caught the faintest hint of his presence when the scent of his elusive cologne and a hint of cigarette smoke would go by me as I went about my daily chores.

I was content knowing that he was still nearby, and so life went on.

Then in December 2010 I became bedridden and was on antibiotics. My recovery was painful and slow. I marked the time sleeping deeply and having moments of great restlessness. I came to grips with so many of my childhood hurts.

Near the end of the month I felt drawn to an old book on one of my bookshelves—a book I had picked up at a secondhand bookstore several years before. The book outlined a path for healing that encouraged the reader to create what is known as a "life path." Basically, what was requested is that the reader document his or her life—every single instance from birth to the present day—and create a life chart. This chart, when completed, would show the "core" or "key" issue confronting one and thus the real reason behind any dis-ease (the lack of ease in the body when illness strikes) or emotional issues.

I began my life path, and by the time I had gotten to when I was age four I found that my key issue was indeed abandonment—an emotionally charged core problem that strikes at the heart of security and that, according to the author, opens the body and soul to all sorts of dis-ease and sadness.

I spent the next few weeks reliving my past—the parts I could have controlled by making other choices, and the parts I'd had absolutely no control over, like being given to my grandparents as an infant.

This time of illness was a soul-wrenching, deeply painful reawakening period, as I confronted and released as much of the past as I could. I learned about forgiving deeply, accepting unconditionally, and becoming peaceful with the knowledge of myself and my vastness of being. I embraced who I was now and released who I had been.

I learned to be grateful on every level for all the things I had taken for granted.

On December 27, 2010, after a particularly rough session of introspection, physical pain, and crying, I fell into a deep sleep.

Instantly I began to dream.

I was at Pleasant View, outside at the back of the house standing by the corner of the building. Dan was with me, and I got the impression that we were waiting for something to happen or someone very important to arrive. It was a balmy summer night. I looked up at the sky. Above us arched a canopy of twinkling starlight. A full moon shone down, burnishing the landscape with a rich, golden light.

I noticed that the back of the house had reverted to the way it was when I was very young. The deck that Dan had built was gone, and in its place the concrete sidewalk of Grandpa's time glowed in the moonlight.

I moved along the house and found that Dan was gone and I was alone.

At the corner by the front of Pleasant View I came to a stop.

The aroma of cigarette smoke accosted my senses.

Alarmed, I peered cautiously around the corner.

A man was sitting at the front of the house.

Here again was change. The porch Dan had built was gone and back in its place was the concrete slab and step that Grandpa had had when I was young and even before, from when a gas station/refreshment stand was here.

The moonlight showed a man in a dark suit with a top hat of silk on his head. He was leaning back on one elbow and smoking a cigarette, the smoke of which curled out and vanished into the misty night.

He didn't turn to me but I knew who he was—Jeremy! And he was dressed in his Sherlock Holmes attire.

I went over to him and he put out the cigarette and turned to me with a smile. Taking off his hat, he placed it beside him.

"Hello, darling. I came because you were hurt. I don't know how much help I can be to you—I'm very tired."

He put his hands on his face, and indeed the tiredness seemed to radiate off him in waves.

I sat down beside him and put my arm around his back and held him, running my hands up to his very short hair and stroking it softly. I couldn't help but notice that he was now heavier, as he had been on some of the later Holmes shows, and his chronological age was the same as when he had passed. The slim and youthful Jeremy who had greeted me at the train station shortly after his death was gone.

In his place was a near-bloated version of my dear friend.

I forgot my present dilemma and became very concerned for him.

"Thank you for coming to me, Jeremy. If you're that tired, maybe we can go inside and you can rest for a while."

"I'd like that," he said, picking up his hat and standing with great difficulty.

I reached for the door, and again it had reverted back to the red screen and then the wooden doors of my youth.

I paused.

"Before we go in, I have to tell you that the house is a mess. Because I've been ill I haven't had much of a chance to clean at all."

"I'm not worried about that. Perhaps just a quick rest and I'll be better."

We went in.

The light in the hallway was on. Inside the house appeared as it does in the present day; however, oddly enough, I sensed that my grandparents were asleep in the bedroom.

Quietly I led Jeremy to the stairs, and he went wearily up. I followed. He went to lie down on one of the twin beds and was soon deeply asleep. I covered him with a blanket and tiptoed away.

Downstairs, I paused and realized that my grandparents hadn't even been awakened by my arrival with Jeremy.

I also wondered where Dan had gone to.

Perplexed, I stood in the hallway and soon woke up.

This dream of Jeremy caused me to contemplate a new idea.

I wondered if it were possible that spirits come to care for us when other spirits cannot.

Jeremy obviously was exhausted by his journey back to Earth to give me comfort—a comfort I greatly appreciated as I dealt again and again over the next few days with the real anguish of letting go of many years of feeling lost and alone and despondent.

Also, the fact that I had somehow sensed that my grandparents were in the house and asleep and yet unable to attend to me for that window of time was another telling point. Because of their advanced age when they left Earth, could the trip back have been even harder on them than on Jeremy, who was, at his passing, at least twenty years younger than either of them? Or had they both moved on to a place or level far distant from where Jeremy was spiritually and could only send their essence back to help me?

This was very puzzling.

Then there was Jeremy's altered physical appearance. The journey to the earth plane seemed to have cost him both his youth and his vigor.

I did not like seeing him so worn out, but I was, at the same time, comforted in knowing that this dear man had sacrificed his energy to come back from one realm to another to be with me and to let me know that he cared and understood despite us being in two different worlds.

As I came closer and closer to healing I found great solace in the knowing that I was never really alone. Those who had loved and cherished me when they were alive did the best they could to intercede and let me know of their love and great concern.

What a joy it was to have that knowledge!

All things continue and never end. It's like a ribbon that stretches across all time and space, uniting and connecting all of us despite the fact that we may exist in different dimensions.

Sometimes during the long winter nights in upstate New York, Dan and I take delight in pulling out one of the old videotapes of Jeremy as Sherlock and watching it. Oddly, this very act can sometimes trigger a dream visit from him—not always, but often.

One night in early 2011 Dan was off from his part-time job for the evening and all our chores were done, so we opted to watch Jeremy in "The Priory School" episode, one of our favorites of the Holmes series.

The next morning Jeremy came to me in another vivid dream.

We were standing in some place of business. It did not seem as though it was here in the United States but rather in the United Kingdom or a nearby country. The atmosphere was almost like a pub—but a pub that was in the early stages of remodeling. There was a highly polished perhaps mahogany bar, and in the distant rooms I could see wooden tables and chairs stacked about. A doorway through which murky sunshine attempted entrance was directly across and in front of me. On a table close by and on the bar were spread what I perceived as architectural drawings and stacks of other papers. I was leaning against the bar and waiting for someone to appear, but I had no idea who that someone might be.

On this occasion I was able to note that I was in my younger, slimmer body self and wearing a floral-print white dress that had been a favorite of mine circa the mid-1960s. My hair was again long and cascaded down past my shoulders. It gave me pause for a few moments to find myself so young and yet with the knowledge of the present time I lived in. But this had happened to me many times before, and I let go of the wondering and continued to observe the place I was in.

I looked up and saw Dan walk past the doorway, pause, come in, and go down a hallway to the left and disappear.

Shortly after Jeremy came into the place—not through any door but by simply appearing. He looked positively wonderful. He was dressed in modern-day clothing, yet he was now appearing quite his slim, youthful self once more. I estimated his age to be somewhere between thirty-five and forty.

He took off his tan and very expensive-looking suit jacket, laid it on the bar, and picked up one of the drawings and tapped it for a few moments before glancing at me.

"Well, hello, darling," he said mentally, laying the drawing down on the bar. "You seem to pop up in the most interesting spots."

"Sorry about that," I said. "I don't seem to be able to control where I'll be when I have these dreams."

"Oh, that's quite all right," he said, going over to the table to look at some other drawings laid out there. "I enjoy having you around. You know I think of you often."

I was so deep in thought about the dichotomies of the dream—not just the fact that I was able to note to Jeremy that I was in fact dreaming but also a few other things as well: Jeremy young and vibrant again yet with the hint of the eternal about him, Dan appearing and walking down the hallway and vanishing, and I young again—that I almost missed the inflection of his words in my mind.

I went over to him and laid my hand on his arm, and he looked up at me, his eyes alight with something I had never seen there.

He turned to me, leaned in, and kissed me tenderly.

Then he said aloud, "I will love you forever."

And I said aloud, "I've loved you since the first day I saw you."

The spell was weaving itself around us. We were joined, I felt, on a level that hearkened back to the verse he had sent me from *The Prophet* a few years before.

He pulled a few of the papers from the table and began a search through them and seemed worried. "Where are the rest of the plans for this business?" he asked aloud, as he rifled through them. "Who has taken them?"

Now it became obvious to me that he was in the process of owning this pub and remodeling it.

He turned to me with near-lightning speed. "You haven't seen the papers I'm talking about, have you, Marilou?"

I assured him I had not, but that I was willing to look if he would describe them to me.

Suddenly, he looked up as if he had heard a sound from very far away.

The door opened by itself and above it a bell rang—a bell that had not been there before when Dan had come in.

Two shadowy figures stood there outlined by the dim light from outside. They could have been either male or female, but I could not ascertain which, as they seemed really to be neither one sex nor the other but rather androgynous—and they also seemed to be waiting. They neither moved deeper into the room nor spoke, but Jeremy seemed to know them.

He pulled on his coat, grabbed a few of the papers, gave me a kiss on the cheek, and said to me, mentally again, "I have to leave for a while. I love you, darling. I'll be back when I can."

He went up to them; they moved to either side of him; and then they all moved out into the light of outdoors and vanished.

I stayed standing by the bar, pondering for a while, and then left myself, waking soon afterward with the glow of the dream enveloping me in a warm cocoon of love.

This amazing dream visit from Jeremy was of particular note as it was indeed a rare blend of past, present, and future, and all the elements had that oh-so-real feeling to them that, to my mind, marks the event in dreamtime as a total experience on all levels of my body, mind, and spirit. Not one detail was left to chance during this time with Jeremy. It was allowed that he was once more his youthful self. Dan moved through the dreamscape, albeit quickly, but as part of my present he was there—perhaps as a gentle reminder of the life I was currently living. I was youthful again, yet with the knowledge of my present self and life. And Jeremy and I had been allowed to share a memorable moment.

I woke up grateful for everything that Heaven allows me to experience in my dreams.

chapter seven

A Plethora of Spirits Dream Visit

Over the years an assortment of spirits have paid me dream visits and allowed me admittance to their worlds. These visits are from regular folks like my father-in-law, all the way to those hallowed members of the literary and religious halls of fame, some of whom have been dead for a hundred years or more. These latter figures from history seem to come to me in regards to my career as a writer, as they are certainly people I have revered since childhood.

I deeply cherish all the visits noted here.

My Father-in-Law

Dan's father was one of those men who had a take-charge attitude about life and business dealings. For many years he was involved deeply in union work and was closely allied with many of the high rollers in the government of our home state, New York.

When I first met him, he and his second wife, Ellen, came upstate from Long Island to visit Dan and me prior to our November wedding in 1988. He was very accepting of me and very happy for his son having fallen in love. We all went out to dinner at a local restaurant, where he regaled us with tales of the things he had done in his youth. Our time together was very nice, and I was heartened by the acceptance I felt from him.

He and Ellen returned for the wedding along with several other relatives, and he was also Dan's best man.

After this we didn't meet again for a year or so, at which time Dan and I went to visit him and Ellen on Long Island. That visit didn't go as smoothly, as it seemed we were intruding on their daily routines.

He was now involved in local government and working as a commissioner as well as still being involved in union business.

Dan and I returned home, glad to be back, and from that time until my father-in-law's passing we had little contact except through cards sent back and forth for birthdays or holidays and the occasional phone call.

On Memorial Day 1995 Dan's father collapsed and died of a heart attack at his home.

Dan was stuck at work, as was I during that year, and so we were unable to make it to the funeral on Long Island.

Yet, oddly enough, the lack of communication among us and our inability to attend his services didn't deter my father-in-law from visiting me, both in dreams and during my waking hours in a sort of mental picture show—a very new experience for me as it was a blend of a spirit visit and a dream visit, and yet I was also cognizant of the here and now.

The first of these "waking picture shows" happened one day when Dan was sitting with me at the dining room table and we were talking about his father.

It was as if the talking about him had summoned him.

Quickly an image of him rose up in my mind. He appeared to be sitting on an unseen box of some sort and was in a place filled with fog-shrouded gray mist. I could clearly see that he was wearing a short-sleeved yellow shirt that was open at the collar, a white T-shirt, and tan slacks. He was sitting with his head in his hands and appeared to be very sad and upset.

He mind-spoke to me that he knew he had died but that he was in this place and he didn't know where it was.

I mentally asked him if he could see or hear anything at all.

He quickly responded, "I hear voices in the distance and I think I hear my mother's voice."

I asked him, "Why don't you go toward your mother's voice?"

He looked up and straight at me. "I can't. I'm too embarrassed for her to see me."

Dan was seated nearby, and as this was unfolding I told him what was going on.

My father-in-law seemed burdened with remorse, yet he was also concerned for his son. "Is Dan okay?" he asked.

I assured him that he was.

"I'm glad he's happy."

He paused and looked up as if listening to voices again.

"Is someone there?" I asked.

"Lots of people are near me, but I can't see them. Just hear them," he replied.

Raised as a Roman Catholic as I was, I wondered if he was in one of those in-between places like Purgatory, where the souls that still need a little bit of help have to reside until they can be admitted to Heaven.

Before I could ask anything further, he was gone.

I thought back to my own near-death experiences and the delightful places I had found myself in. I considered all the other dream visits from departed loved ones. Obviously, this place where my father-in-law resided was totally unlike anything I had ever seen.

Apparently, the fact was that not all spirits go to a balmy summer place on the other side where joyous crowds wait for one's arrival at a train station, nor do all who pass end up picnicking on sunny meadows or share convivial times with loved ones.

For a portion of time, some apparently become stuck in a joyless void.

I was very concerned for my father-in-law, but I was also wise enough to know that the basic personality of the deceased survives death, and thus I had every reassurance that he would find his way to the place where he would be able to reside in peace and harmony.

After several other waking dream visits from him that were basically of the same theme as the first (concern for his son, his inability to move from the gray area—or desire not to because of not wanting to meet up with his mother), my father-in-law came to me during my sleeping hours.

It was about eight months after his passing.

He was still in the gray area, but this time he was not seated, but standing and looking off in the distance and then back at me.

He was dressed the same and still appeared to be his chronological earth age.

I mentally asked him what was going on.

He put his finger to his lips and said, "Shhh! Just a minute."

I listened with him but heard nothing.

He pointed off through the gray mist.

I could now plainly see distorted human shapes walking about.

"That's where I need to go," he whispered.

"Is your mother there?" I asked.

"Yes. And she forgives me."

I urged him to go.

"Please tell my son I love him."

I promised I would.

He turned and walked into the grayness that now seemed to have changed to a blue-gray mist that was thinning and appeared to be lit from within by a bright light. I watched as several of the humanoid forms came up to him and surrounded him.

I stood and observed for a few minutes. I felt that he was going to be okay and I left, waking shortly afterward.

I told Dan about the dream, and he seemed to be at peace with his father's being able to leave the gray area behind and go forward in his journey on the other side.

The Stowe Family and Mark Twain

Writing the biography of William H. Gillette brought me deeply into his world, especially during the time I was researching the exclusive Nook Farm neighborhood in Hartford, Connecticut, where Will had resided as a boy and a young man. The neighborhood had been a sort of closed community wherein such notables as Harriet Beecher Stowe, Samuel L. Clemens (Mark Twain), and, in later years, the well-known actress Katharine Hepburn resided.

Mrs. Stowe was the author who wrote the insightful anti-slavery book *Uncle Tom's Cabin* in 1852, a book that exposed the horrible reality of slavery to millions of readers. Harriet and her sisters and brothers would go on to forge a path through the landmine social issues of the day, which included fighting for the right of women to vote, spiritualism, and abolitionism.

Mark Twain was an author and lecturer who looked at the world and its circumstances with a sharp wit and an eagle eye. I had admired him since I was very young.

During my last year or so of really digging into the completion of the biography, it seemed that the research I was doing awakened the spirits of several of these famous people and also allowed me a sort of time-travel dream visit back to Nook Farm when those marvelous people were still alive.

During this dreamtime I appeared to have simply walked into the scene.

It was a sunny summer day, and the scent of flowers blooming, birds singing, and carriages drawn by horses pervaded my senses. I paused for a moment and let the realization sink in that I was no longer in my own time but had magically been transported back to the nineteenth century.

I reveled in the moment. I closed my eyes and just let pure enjoyment rush over me.

Soon I moved forward.

I heard the joyful shrieks of children and looked up.

I saw the familiar Mark Twain house and on the lawn playing chase was none other than Mark Twain, walking about while his young daughters played around him. He was dressed in casual attire and was smoking a cigar, the aroma of which wafted to my nostrils.

He looked up at me, and somehow we knew one another.

He waved and yelled out, "Hello, Marilou!"

I yelled back, "Hello, Mr. Clemens. Lovely day!"

The girls ran up to him and surrounded him, pulling him forward. He waved goodbye to me over his shoulder and went into his house.

It was a beautiful, beautiful scene I had been allowed to see, and I will cherish it always.

All around me shadow figures moved, the ghosts of those who had once called this place home. They seemed to have purpose and a firm destination in mind as they walked along. They had no cognizance of my presence, and as they did not interfere in my time, I did not interfere in theirs.

I turned and looked to my right and left.

I was aware of the fact that Harriet Beecher Stowe had moved into the Chamberlin House (the one that is now preserved as her home), and I also knew that I was expected to be there soon to help her with her cooking.

I was about to turn, when up the sidewalk came a portly man in a dark suit of the day. His shoulder-length light hair seemed to stand out to me.

He drew closer.

He had his hands behind his back and was striding along toward me at a pretty good clip. He appeared to be in deep thought.

When he drew even with me he paused, smiled at me, and mind-talked, "Hello, Marilou. Enjoy your visit. Oh, and if you get a chance, do visit the flower gardens and take note of the hummingbirds there."

After he moved on, I realized that he was none other than Reverend Henry Ward Beecher, younger brother of Harriet. His life was remarkable for being the charismatic preacher who enthralled the congregation at Plymouth Church in Brooklyn, New York, with his sermons. He was a staunch abolitionist and women's rights advocate who commanded the world's stage when he was brought to trial for adultery and was found innocent by both his church and in civil court in Brooklyn after his accusers were found to be of an unsavory and greedy character.

Henry had a stroke and died in 1887 at age seventy-three, several years after the trial, but here he appeared to me to be in his mid-forties.

I watched him walk toward Harriet's house, and I followed.

I went up to the door of the house and walked in.

There were no locked doors at Nook Farm, and friends and neighbors were always able to make free use of one another's homes.

In the kitchen I found Harriet, who also appeared younger than she was when she died, about fiftyish. She was with another woman, who I thought was perhaps a cook or maid. The cook was standing at a counter with her back to me and didn't turn around. Harriet was leaning over a wooden table and covered in flour. She looked up when she saw me come in, smiled in recognition, and motioned to a cloth-covered bowl on another table nearby. Having made many loaves of bread, I knew this was dough rising. Mrs. Stowe mind-spoke to me that I could be of help if I would knead the dough and put it in loaf pans and place the pans in the oven. Next to the bowl was a floured board with all the bread pans lined up.

The room was extremely warm and full of the scents of good things cooking. Most outstanding to me were the enticing aromas of sage and rosemary.

As I rolled up my sleeves I looked down and saw that I was dressed in a sort of long tan skirt with a matching blouse and that I was in my present physical form. I ignored my attire and began to do as Mrs. Stowe had instructed.

I was so happy to be working with her and briefly wondered if I would be staying for dinner. I was truly hoping to talk with her about my writing and how I could improve it.

The cook came over from where she had been washing vegetables and looked at me.

She so clearly resembled one of my best friends in the present that I almost gasped.

She smiled at me cheerfully and went back to scrubbing carrots and potatoes.

Henry came into the kitchen and grabbed a carrot and smiled at me again before leaving.

Sadly, I didn't get to stay for dinner.

It seemed that my time in the past was to be a visit that ended all too soon.

I woke up from my deep slumber feeling as if I had returned from a long and successful journey—a bit tired and totally at peace. In the morning I shared my dream with Dan. The next time I spoke to my friend, I told her about the cook's uncanny resemblance to her. Her response: "I could just visualize that!"

Mark Twain Again

During a visit that Dan and I paid to Hartford a couple of years ago, we had the opportunity to tour the Mark Twain House.

As soon as I entered the house I felt that old familiar *zing* of recognition, as if I had walked through that door on many occasions in the past.

As the tour progressed to the upstairs and to the bedroom of his daughters, I began to feel somewhat closed in. Not exactly a panic attack but something more akin to that near-prickly feeling of anticipation whenever I am touched by a spirit.

I stepped away from the tour slightly and into the hallway. Behind me was the girls' room. The tour guide was somewhat upset and took a moment to caution me to "come back to the group."

Just as he did this, a girl's voice screamed my name in my head, "Marilou!" I turned and watched in awe as a dark shadow flew out of the bedroom, headed for the stairs, and vanished through a wall. After I recovered my equilibrium I thought this might be the spirit of Susy Clemens, Twain's daughter who had died in the Hartford house in 1896 at age twenty-four of spinal meningitis.

I acknowledged the spirit's mental shout and moved on with the tour and did not see or hear from her again.

Mark Twain and I had a marvelous dream visit shortly after I began working on the biography again about a year ago.

It seems that a writer is always willing to encourage another of the same ilk.

Once more, it was summertime. On this dream occasion I found I was inside Mark's home in Hartford, and though it was somewhat altered from what I remembered after the tour Dan and I had taken, I knew where I was because I looked out the window and across the lawn to Harriet's home.

Out on that lawn I watched as numerous shadow figures glided about and, as usual, I could discern no real features of sex or dress.

I was seated at a table in the front room with several piles of paper in front of me. And again I was in my present physical form and dressed in a present-day attire of blouse, suit jacket, and black slacks. I looked down and read some of the pages, noting that it was the biography I was working on.

I heard a dog bark from somewhere inside the house and looked up. In through the doorway came Samuel Clemens. He was now in his familiar white linen suit and puffing on a cigar.

He came right over to the table and tapped the closest pile of papers very meaningfully, and I looked up at him.

He mind-spoke, "You know you have to get this thing done soon, don't you?"

He and I continued to gaze into one another's eyes for a few seconds as I gauged the seriousness of his words. I was feeling somewhat ashamed that I was so behind in completing the book—a book many had contributed to before their own passing.

I replied, "I'll do my best, Mr. Clemens."

"Good enough," he said, and then turned abruptly and left the room.

I stayed seated at the table and dealt with my own puzzlement.

How was it that a man of the caliber of Samuel Clemens cared about a biography I was writing? Compared to the things he had written—things that had more than stood the test of time—this single book that would chronicle the life of a young man he had given a start to seemed to me to be small potatoes.

As my grandfather had done, I cogitated on the deeper meaning of the visit.

I was very grateful to Mr. Clemens, because this communication gave me yet another hint of the afterlife and that those who reside there who are of a similar mindset as mine are interested in things such as books that impact them.

It was a precious connection to the past I loved, and so I looked upon it as a sweet and dear moment I will treasure always.

Though many of the original buildings at Nook Farm are gone, it appeared to me that this didn't matter in the spirit world. Dearly loved homes seem to survive in the form in which their occupants remembered them during their earthly tenure, and the spirits who reside there seem content to abide for eternity in familiar surroundings.

In any event I am so grateful for their visits to me in my dreams and the allowance of being able to share their days in the past. Truly, creative souls continue on and encourage others to delve into that space where inspiration holds sway and the story is born to be shared with all.

My Paternal Grandmother

I never met my paternal grandmother, as she passed away before I was born. However, during one of my visits to my father and stepmother I was given some photos of her. Her name was Mabel, and she'd had a twin sister who predeceased her, reportedly of a "broken heart."

The black-and-white photos showed a somewhat chunky woman walking sedately along or lying on the ground beside a friendly dog. I did not know what age she was in the photos, but to me her demeanor seemed sad, remote, and careworn, as if she were getting ready to leave the world and all its many troubles behind. Despite her being a true blood relation to me, I felt no tug of recognition, no feelings of emotional attachment or connection to her—any more than I had toward my biological father. When I looked

Marilou's paternal grandmother, Mabel

into Mabel's eyes in those photos, it was as if I were looking at nothing more than the face of a stranger.

Again, here was a broken link that didn't resonate with my soul in any way.

However, I was to learn, a few weeks after bringing those photos home, that Grandmother Mabel had maintained an ethereal connection to me and was about to cross the barrier between our worlds to meet me—her unmet granddaughter.

Suffice it to say that the details of this dream were somewhat confusing to me at first, but then things righted themselves and I spent a not-unpleasant time in Mabel's company as well as relishing the added bonus of a visit from the shadows of my ancestors.

Oddly, this dream took place at Pleasant View in the present day, outside on the lawn that lies between the garage and a small shed that had once been the outhouse and was later a tool/feed shed.

It was a sunny and warm summer day, and the smell of newly mown grass on Grandpa's lawn was the first thing that tantalized my senses. I looked around and saw that the landscape of my dream, as usual, had altered to the past with my form being of the present. This made sense, as Mabel would have "watched" me grow and would easily recognize me in my present form.

The air was permeated with the sweet aroma of Grandpa's flowers: peonies, roses clinging to a trellis, multihued gladiolus, hollyhocks, black-eyed Susans—all perfectly layered and giving off their own particular fragrances. Bees and hummingbirds buzzed and flitted about the blossoms. Robins hopped on the lawn in front of me—seemingly unworried about my presence.

I also sensed rather than saw that my grandparents were somewhere nearby.

I felt the approach of a presence. It came to me as a sort of warm, wafting feeling of an unfamiliar *nearness*.

I turned to face it.

From directly in front of me, and out of a golden-brown mist that swirled with energy, came a short, somewhat heavyset woman with auburn hair. Behind her were the shapes and forms of quite a few other people, but they remained in the shadows and I could not make out any distinguishing characteristics of face, sex, or clothing.

The woman stepped up to me and looked me in the eyes, her gaze quizzical and bold with uncertainty. It was as if she were assessing me to see if I would flinch from her presence or if I would stand my ground.

I stayed still and we looked at one another closely for several moments.

Of course I recognized her from the photographs I had just seen a few days before. It was Mabel, my paternal grandmother.

She mind-spoke to me, her voice raspy and yet calm.

"Hello, Marilou. Do you know who I am?"

"Yes." I answered quickly. "You are my grandmother, my father's mother."

"That's right."

"Do you know why I'm here?"

I had to admit I didn't.

She walked slowly around me, still assessing. Then she stopped again in front of me.

"I came because I felt it was time for you and I to meet."

As soon as she spoke, the shadow figures moved from inside the golden-brown light and began to take on form and distinctive shapes, and I could easily make out who was male and who was female. They were an odd array, dressed in suits, commonplace dresses, and work clothes; one woman appeared in Native American attire. I could see about thirty of them surrounding me. They seemed, like Mabel, to be curious about me and yet hesitant about coming too close.

Mabel ignored them for the time being and looked around at the Pleasant View property.

"Are you happy here?" she asked.

I was unsure of exactly what she was asking. Did she want to know if I was happy on Earth or happy here at Pleasant View?

"I'm sorry," I said, "I don't understand what you mean."

"Are you happy with your life the way it is?"

"Yes. Why?" I responded.

"Just a question I've always wanted to ask you. You know this is the only chance we will get to talk until the time comes when you pass over. Then you might not want to be with me."

I thought it interesting that she somehow knew that I felt no genuine connection to her and in fact would prefer to be in the company of my grandparents on the other side.

I didn't want to hurt her feelings—realizing, of course, that she had just made an incredible effort to come and see me.

"I'm glad you came to see me today and that we can spend some time together."

This seemed to soothe her, and she smiled at me kindly.

"You're a good girl, Marilou. A credit to your grandparents and your upbringing. I'm at peace knowing that you have had a good life and that you turned out all right."

"Thank you," I said.

After this emotional moment, Mabel seemed to fade somewhat into the misty brownish-gold area. As she faded the shadow people moved closer to me. I could smell the antiquity that clung to them as they came within a hair's breadth of touching me. Indeed, it was like being in the attic of a very old house—an elusive cobwebby scent of age and time that is unmistakable. My grandmother's voice echoed from inside the void. "These are your ancestors, Marilou. They also wanted to meet you. Treat them with the respect they deserve."

I stood while the shadow figures formed two circles around me. They suddenly seemed to vibrate with an incredible energy. I reasoned that perhaps because they had been in spirit so long they operated on a different wavelength than the spirits I was used to.

I stayed still. The "old ones," as I called them, moved about then. Every once in a while I felt a small *zing* go through my body as if one of them had touched me quickly and backed away. It was not at all unpleasant and seemed to transfer to me knowledge and understanding of my roots and my past, present, and future.

Gradually the golden-brown mist swirled as if a giant wind had come up. The images of the old ones faded, came back into my sight, and faded again, until I found I was standing all alone on the lawn in a place between then and now and in a form both of spirit and physical.

The birds sang, the sun shone down, the wind moved gently through the leaves of the lawn's maple. I looked up at the blue sky and thanked my grandmother and the old ones for their visit and for the connection they had shared with me that allowed me to be in touch with my ancestral self and the ones who had given me life.

"Gramma" Irene

I have never really believed in coincidence. Even as a very young child I marveled at the timing of things—how a person was in a right or wrong place at a right or wrong time so that they experienced a really good or a really bad thing. Such a fact was the timing of Edward Junior's death—*why*, I had pondered for many years, at that precise moment that he crossed the road did a car come along and hit him, when he had been going back and forth all day watching a road crew thawing out pipes at a neighbor's house across the street?

Another bit of timing—on the good-experience side of things—was my meeting with Butch. If I hadn't been visiting my neighbor's horse that day and if his cousins hadn't brought him across the street to see the horse, would he and I have ever met?

Similar factors exist with every single person I have encountered during my lifetime, whether that person be in my life to share love or to teach me a harsh lesson.

The randomness of events has always seemed, at least to me, very well ordered to occur precisely when the events were supposed to occur.

Finding Irene was one of those events—she was definitely an angel I needed and a true friend of the heart whose wisdom was beyond reproach.

One spring day about five years ago Dan and I got home from a country ride and some shopping. The message light on the phone was blinking, so I played the messages. One of them was a wrong number—but it would really, it turned out, be an incredibly *right* number for me at that particular time of my life.

The sweet, quavering voice on the machine was obviously that of an elderly lady. She was asking to leave a message for a friend in my hometown, and she gave the full name of her friend and left her phone number.

I immediately called her back. Her name was Irene, and she was widowed and lived alone in an apartment complex about a half-hour from our home. She and I talked and talked that first day and found we had so much in common.

At the time of that first talk she was in her late eighties. She told me she had become wheelchair-bound a year or so before, after falling on her way into her apartment on a bitterly cold winter day. She had lain in a snowbank and not been found for several hours. Frostbite had taken a toll on her legs and one of her arms. She'd had a twin sister who had died not so long ago, and Irene had never had any children. She had relatives who lived at a great distance, and she was soon to be a great-aunt—an event that would bring her both joy and sorrow. After the baby was born, she loved to look at the photos of her new great-niece, but she knew and spoke it aloud that she would "never be able to meet the child or hold her, because I will be gone."

Still, she kept up her hope of a visit with that most-desired-to-cuddle-with baby girl.

Irene and I eventually made plans to meet.

Dan and I drove to the apartment complex and got a little lost, but eventually, with Irene's help after we called her on our cell phone, we were at her door.

When she opened the door, seated in her wheelchair, I went to my knees and fell into her arms and we held one another closely—as if we had known one another for ages.

I dubbed her "Gramma" Irene, and she just loved to be called that.

Irene was a tall, thin, aristocratic-looking woman with curly white hair and piercing blue eyes. As it was nearing Easter, I brought her some baked goods—slices of apple pie and pumpkin pie and real whipped cream. She was overjoyed by that, as she said she didn't get very much food or dessert of the homemade variety. She directed me to the cups and plates in her cupboard while she made coffee to go with the dessert. We all sat down and dug in and thoroughly enjoyed being together in her cozy kitchen nook.

Irene and I spoke on the phone almost every other day. On many of these occasions she told me of her great desire to die and to be at peace and reunited with her husband, sister, mother, and father—all of whom she missed so deeply.

An astute businesswoman who had worked for many years at a local factory, she was very much up to date on the politics of working in an office. At the office where I worked things were not so good, and I often sought her advice on such dilemmas. Her perceptive advice was: "Leave that job and write your books full time. That's what your real calling in life is."

As it would turn out, a few years later I would take her advice. I have never looked back.

Irene and I shared so much of our life's journey with one another. She was the wise woman I needed in my life at that time, and I honored a convivial universe that brought her accidentally on purpose into my life.

Because I was raised by my grandparents and am knowledgeable of the ways of the elderly, Irene and I understood one another perfectly.

She shared her extraordinary beginning with me.

She had lived in a different county a few miles distant from me and had been born there almost ninety years ago. As it happened, the story of her birth would bring into my life and dreamscape yet another historical figure—a historical figure she had lived just up the road from during her growing-up years.

As Irene told it, she and her identical twin sister had been born prematurely. Because it was winter, the advice given was to "put the babies in the oven to keep them warm."

So, Irene and her twin were put in a blanket-lined pot in the woodstove oven to keep them warm.

One of their neighbors was none other than author/ naturalist John Burroughs. He heard about the birth of the girls and, according to Irene, "just had to come and see us" because twins were such an "oddity." Irene's mother told her that he was amazed at how tiny they were and that he thoroughly enjoyed meeting them. He returned to visit the girls a few more times just prior to his death.

Irene led a quietly rural life on the family farm. She adored her parents and her family and the joy of running through the fields and tending to the farm animals—so in effect a great deal of her life was similar to mine.

When I completed my first book and it was published, Irene was ecstatic and constantly urged me to make this my life's work.

A while after the book publication, Irene was taken to a hospital and given a series of tests. It was found that she had colon cancer and that her days were numbered. It wasn't long after the diagnosis that she was moved by her family into a care facility not far from her apartment. Dan and I visited her there on a warm near-spring day. She was up and about in her wheelchair, and we shared much good conversation. I brought her a copy of my book and an angel coverlet I had sewn for her. She gave me a brass tea set to go with the afghan she had given me to "remember" her by.

In 2006 the entire area that includes the counties in which Irene and Dan and I resided was hit by massive floods, and travel became impossible as roadways washed out, interstate bridges collapsed, and people lost their homes and belongings. It was a disaster of unprecedented proportions for this area, never before seen during my lifetime or Irene's. During this horrible time, I kept in touch with Irene by phone and letter. Somehow, after this situation was over, time slipped away from me and I was busy with book signings and travel with Dan.

One day I called Irene and she was very angry, a state of being I had never experienced with her. She railed at the fact that she had such a disease and that it was overtaking her. She railed at the fact that she had grown old so quickly. She told me, "Old age isn't for sissies, Marilou." And I believed her then and I believe her now.

After she calmed down a bit, we shared our "I love you"s and I hung up.

Two weeks later I read her obituary. She had at last gotten her wish to die.

She was eighty-nine years of age.

Oh, how I very much missed our talks. Knowing that she was just a phone call away with her sage advice about life and its circumstances, joys, and sorrows had been an undeniable comfort. Much like Jeremy, Irene had been a true soul friend whom I had counted on to be there forever.

Dan and I went to the service the family had arranged for her at her husband's gravesite. She had been cremated—not something she had wanted—and her ashes were placed atop her husband's remains.

I knew Irene would not be happy about this cremation thing at all, because she had told me when she was taken to the care facility that she had her burial dress all picked out.

A few weeks later she was in my dreams and, as I had thought, she was more than a little upset, though glad to be free of her physical body and of the pain of her illness.

Oddly enough, the location in the dream was the office where I was employed as a secretary, and it happened in the waiting room. I thought the setting was somehow appropriate on many levels—yet the most striking to me was that it was a *waiting* room, and I knew at that point in my life that I was the one "waiting" to break away from the mundane life of an office worker and leap into my life as a writer. She apparently was "waiting" to be able to travel to the next level of her new life. In any event, Irene, who had been constantly updated on what was going on in my personal and work life, had chosen that particular dreamscape with some amount of forethought.

It would be our one and only dream meeting.

I was standing in the waiting room, and it was obvious to me that the office was either closed for the day or hadn't opened yet. There was no one else around, but the office lights were on and all the machines were humming to life. I could distinctly hear the fax machine as a document of some sort was being delivered. While that was occurring, the phone rang and stopped after about four rings as the answering machine picked up. Then all was quiet.

I was able to look down at my body and see that I was dressed in my office attire of jacket, black slacks, and loafers.

I waited patiently, knowing that someone was on their way to me—yet I had no idea who it was.

Irene appeared in front of me as if out of nowhere.

Though it was late autumn she was dressed in spring colors of light blue with a white top and skirt. She looked as she had when I had first met her and before the illness that took her life had manifested.

"Marilou!" she said to me mentally. "How I've missed our talks."

"Me too, Gramma Irene," I answered.

She didn't waste any time getting to the matter that was disturbing her. This was typical Irene—though a Christian woman, she cut to the chase and had a sense of judgment and targeted resolve that could melt steel.

"Did you see what they did to me?"

"You mean the cremation?"

"Yes!"

"I know. I thought you had wanted to be buried."

"I most certainly did!"

She seemed to pause and stew over this for a moment. I took advantage of her silence.

"But are you okay?"

"Oh, I'm fine now. Glad to be rid of that body that held me down."

I looked at her. Suddenly, I realized she was standing up! How had I missed that?

In my brief time with her I had only seen her in her wheelchair, pulling herself along by using her good foot to motivate around her apartment and the hospital room.

"Irene," I said, "you're standing up!"

"Yes. I've been able to do that ever since I left."

"That is amazing!" I said.

"Have you found your husband and family yet?" I asked.

"Not yet. That comes later, so I'm told. I'm looking forward to it."

One part of my sleeping, rational mind must have found this perplexing.

"I thought that when you died all your loved ones came to get you," I said.

"Not always. Sometimes you have to wait a bit."

Now, I got the parallel with the "waiting" room.

She spoke no more of her cremation and, in fact, seemed at peace with it, as if the voicing of her displeasure had taken some of the sting out of it.

Her image began to fade, and I wished that I could hug her goodbye, but that feeling of a force field separating us was present. I knew that it would not be allowed, as she was newly in spirit and was about to transform or, as I now call it, youthen.

"You get on with your writing, Marilou. We'll meet again when it's time."

"I will, Irene. I promise. Thank you for being my friend and my 'Gramma' for a while."

"You're welcome, dear."

"I love you, Irene."

"I love you, too."

Then she was gone and I was alone.

The office seemed to shut down then. The lights dimmed and went out. The machines no longer clattered to life.

I moved out into the hallway in my semi-spirit yet strangely physical body and woke up thankful that Irene was at peace.

I had, during my time with Irene, begun to give her angel statues as gifts, and these she displayed about her living room.

That December, Dan and I went to the cemetery where she was buried, and I brushed away the snow that had accumulated on her grave and placed there a small ornamental Christmas tree and a little ceramic angel.

It seemed the right thing to do as I honored the angel friend and "Gramma" she had been to me during her brief yet fulfilling time in my life.

Naturalist John Burroughs

There is an old Buddhist saying I cling to, and it fits with all of the people and spirits I have met in my dream life, both historical and otherwise: "When the student is ready, the teacher will appear." And Mr. Burroughs was definitely a true mentor to me while I was contemplating my first writing project.

Irene's coming into my life and sharing her stories of John Burroughs with me was truly perfect timing.

And despite his very short dream visit with me, he was also to become one of my great spiritual teachers.

Right after Irene's mention of John Burroughs and of his kindness and concern for her and her sister, I began to do some quick research on the man.

It wasn't long before I was as immersed in his being as I was in William Gillette's, and again I felt that I had found a kindred spirit who would eventually traverse the landscape of my dreams and visit me in spirit shortly after Dan and I were allowed to tour his home in the county near mine.

John Burroughs was born on the family farm near Roxbury, New York, on April 3, 1837, and was the seventh of ten children. During his youth he was a keen observer of nature and the habits of the wildlife that surrounded him. He took particular note of the birds, marveling at their springtime returns and habits. Eventually he grew restless and yearned for something more. He wanted to be educated in far more than what his local school could teach.

Again, the similarities between William Gillette and Jeremy Brett come to the fore. John's father was, by most accounts, not at all supportive of him wanting to enhance his life with education, and so young John set off at age seventeen to acquire what he could not in the mountains and valleys near his home village.

John was to achieve his dream of becoming educated. He would go on to be a teacher, an essayist, and an author of many books dealing with nature, and eventually he was credited as one of the original conservationists of his time. He would marry his first love, Ursula, and then after Ursula's death and toward the end of his life, he would find true love with another woman admirer, Clara Barrus. He had a son, Julian.

John Burroughs would become close friends with such notables as Henry Ford and Thomas A. Edison. It was rumored that Edison was, by 1920, involved in the invention of what was to be termed a "ghost box," or an apparatus that would enable one to communicate with the dead. Henry Ford and Edison were both believers in reincarnation. In 1927 Ford was quoted as saying, "For thirty years I have leaned toward the theory of reincarnation. It seems a most reasonable philosophy and explains many things."

However, Burroughs had a somewhat different belief about his own soul's survival after death. He believed he would "not be imprisoned in that grave where you are to bury my body." He was attuned to the belief that after his death his soul would become a part of nature. He did not ascribe to reincarnation, but he believed, in effect, that he would always be here and inhabiting the earthly plane, not going anywhere at all, never being re-embodied in the physical again—just invisible and present. It was an interesting concept.

After Irene introduced me to Burroughs, my fascination with him grew day by day. When I had the glimmer of an idea to write an article about him, I contacted the historical society in Roxbury, and Dan and I went to Woodchuck Lodge and were given the aforementioned personal guided tour. I later found that photos I had taken that day could be described as "ghostly," as there was a manifestation in several of the upstairs shots.

On one visit there I went to sit at a picnic table near the back kitchen door. Thunder began to rumble over the massive range of the Catskill Mountains visible far across the valley and meadows. I sat and wrote down some inspirational words for my first book in a spiral notebook. Nearby, honey bees buzzed in a flowering bush, birds chirped and flitted about me, and chipmunks scurried through the lawns. The sweet aroma of lilacs pervaded all. I immersed myself in the persona of John Burroughs and felt, during that sweet nearly summer day, that he somehow slipped into my soul and began to talk to me of bygone days that had my being yearning to go back in time and sit with him at the table and have a conversation about writing and nature and the beauty that surrounds us but so often goes unseen.

The thunder rumbled closer, and the time at Woodchuck Lodge had to be cut short so that Dan and I could drive down the road a piece, park, and head up to Burroughs' gravesite near the massive rock he called "Boyhood Rock." We wanted to beat the storm if at all possible. The gravesite is through a small field and up a meandering little muddy trail. On all sides there are meadows with stone-piled fences and forest glens where sunshine and shadow play tag with one another.

While the thunder rumbled closer still, I climbed up onto Boyhood Rock and sat looking out over the incredible vista. Just below me was Burroughs' grave with greenery growing all over it, as if hiding it from view. I sat there and cast back in time to the days when a John Burroughs of about ten or so would have climbed up where I was sitting and stood facing the landscape of his home, full of vigor and joy, running through his days on a path to respect and fame.

I came away from Burroughs' home and gravesite that afternoon feeling the peacefulness of the place seeping deep into my heart and soul. Truly, I carried home with me a bit of John's essence.

I knew he had only the very best of intentions for me, and I welcomed him and his muse into my life. I continuously thought about him and the way he had used words to convey the beauty of his surroundings. He was an inspiring being that seemed never to leave my side, especially as I laid out the framework for my first book. I often thought I could hear his gentle, chiding voice urging me to substitute one word for another as I wrote.

By the time I had "met" John Burroughs, he had been in spirit for well over eighty years; he died on March 29, 1921, while on his way home on a train from the West Coast.

One night, about a year after I first visited John's home and gravesite, I had a vivid dream of him. Oddly, he seemed to be cognizant of present worldly affairs as well as other things.

The dream landscape was on the lawn near Woodchuck Lodge and then somehow drifted to the gravesite. He was sitting on the front steps of his home, which now looked to be in finer shape than it was in my time. A black-and-white cat sat nearby. John had not youthened from the pictures I had seen of him taken just prior to his death, and appeared here with white hair and a long white beard. I walked up the lawn and stood in front of him. He did not seem in the least put off by my presence, and in fact it appeared as though he had known I was coming.

He mind-spoke to me.

"Come on up and have a rest," he said, petting the cat. "I've been taking a bit of time to myself." He patted the step one down from him, and I went over and sat.

I noted that even though the sun was shining quite fiercely on us, the air was cool and refreshing with a soft, gentle breeze blowing about. There was also an aroma of dusty age I can only describe as a deep oldness that emanated from Mr. Burroughs. It reminded me of the closed-up attic at Pleasant View after I had gone into it on a hot summer's day.

"How is your writing coming along?" he asked with mind-talk.

"It is going okay. I have a few spots I need to go over again and redo, but it will go to the publisher soon."

He seemed glad to hear this and nodded slowly as if digesting the news.

"Writing can be cathartic as well as lonely at times. I am heartened to know that you are progressing well with the book."

The cat ran off to chase a blue jay that was sprinting about a nearby bush.

John leaned back. "The world has changed a great deal since I walked here."

I acknowledged that it had.

"Too much war and turmoil now. I am glad I am not around to deal with it."

I was about to remark that he had lived through World War I and the Civil War before that, but then I sensed that he was no longer interested in the topic and didn't want to discuss world affairs any longer.

A companionable stillness fell between us.

I also felt no more need for words. I turned as he did, and we both sat on the steps and looked out over the beautiful vista before us—a mountain range that seemed to soar into the sky and the tops of each peak burnished with golden sunshine. A few clouds drifted lazily by, throwing the trees on the tops of those distant hills into shadow for a brief moment as if a giant hand had been laid there and then removed. It was the same scene I witnessed when Dan and I visited there. The only difference was that the field before us in dreamscape was not overgrown with trees and briars and other greenery. Here the path to the distance was clear and pure. Even the air smelled cleaner and more fortifying.

John stood, and I did as well.

"Time for me to go," he said. "But you may come back and visit anytime you like. I'll always be here if you need me."

He stepped up onto the porch and simply vanished.

As I watched, the lodge slowly, slowly took on the appearance I knew it to have in the present day.

I seemed to somehow travel to the gravesite. It was eerily still as I stood looking at his grave.

He did not reappear but mind-spoke to me from somewhere beyond my ken: "I'm not really here anymore, Marilou. Just my bones and nothing else."

I turned and walked down the path, through the field, and down the road, and got into my car and drove off.

That was the only time John Burroughs ever visited me in my dreams, but it was a memorable dream because of the serenity that seemed to linger.

After this I purchased the entire set of his books and began reading them back at Pleasant View, while sitting at a picnic table where the old henhouse had once stood. It seemed appropriate somehow, because when I was a young child I would go up to that building with a couple of my favorite books and a flashlight and sit on an upturned bucket and read the chickens to sleep as they sat on their roosts.

During those spring, summer, and late autumn days, I got to know John Burroughs and walked in his world through his beautiful writing. I felt what he felt, saw with my mind's eye what he seen, and marveled at all of nature that he had so keenly observed and recorded.

His writing was a great help to me in getting in touch with my own voice as I completed my first book.

He was a remarkable man who contributed so much to the world of then and now.

I am very honored to have met him in dreamtime and to have had him as my temporary muse and mentor as I embarked on my path as a writer.

As the years have turned over onto one another and various personages such as John Burroughs and the residents of William Gillette's Nook Farm neighborhood have been kind enough to allow me admittance to their world, I find that I have developed a higher sense of mission. It seems that each one of these people occupied a niche and had a job to do even after death.

To me, that is fascinating.

How would the world have fared without Mark Twain's *Adventures of Huckleberry Finn*, *The Adventures of Tom Sawyer*, or any of his other books? What of the plays William Gillette wrote and acted in, amazing thousands all across the globe? How about Harriet Beecher Stowe and her *Uncle Tom's Cabin*, which brought the rancid face of slavery into the light for millions—all of these spirits from the lowest to the highest echelons all have one thing in common: they gave of themselves so that humankind was better for their having been here.

When we touch the souls of others and they touch ours—no matter which dimension we hail from—it is a miracle to be cherished forever.

chapter eight

Beloved Pets Visit in Spirit and Dreams

There has always been a great deal of contention about the continued existence of the soul of a pet surviving physical death. Most of this debate centers around proving that pets—or any animals—actually have a soul that can migrate from life to death and remain intact as human souls can. And the thought spirals into the wonderment about where those animal souls go after physical death.

Do they go to people Heaven, or is there a special Heaven for animals? Do their souls remain intact as the sweet cat or dog or hamster that you knew and loved, or does each individual animal blend and become part of some cosmic oneness of being, so that, for example, all cats who die merge into a great catness consciousness? Or are pets that pass on somehow able to avoid this merging of like souls so that they can return to the earth plane to assure a much loved and missed human that they are okay?

My experience has been that the answer to the last question is "yes."

The abiding and hopeful thought is that if a human's soul can exist after death, then why not the soul of a pet? Those who take the time to gaze into the eyes of a dog or cat can clearly see the intelligence there—and, to my mind, a soul looking back at me that mirrors my own. Something everlasting shines from those innocent eyes that has always said to my mind, "I am as eternal as you are, and I will never leave you because of the love that binds us together forever."

Yes, there is intelligence in the eyes of animals, and I believe in my heart that there is a place for every single living thing in paradise. I hearken back to the dream visit I had during my college days when I went on that amazing flying dream to paradise, to that summer meadow where the picnicking was going on. I flew alongside birds of all kinds. In the field below me were rabbits gamboling about and deer grazing. Dogs and cats nestled on blankets with their families or chased one another through the grass. The place was alive with animals. I couldn't see them, but perhaps there were even ants parading around the perimeters of the blankets hoping for a tasty crumb to fall.

Some may be skeptical, and that is allowed; however, again, I can only elaborate about the interactions I have had with my beloved pets that are now in spirit form.

As a very young child I knew the joy of curling my baby fingers into the soft fur of a bunny rabbit and deriving from that small presence the comfort of knowing that I was not alone.

Later years with my grandparents would find me befriending the baby chicks we raised for eggs and meat. By the time I was five, a stray cat Grandpa and I christened Puss-in-Boots, because he so enjoyed the cat food of the same name, would come into our lives.

After Puss came Thomas J. Kat, a golden boy cat with startling green eyes. In order of appearance were cats Midnight, Bootsie, Muffin, Brutus, Quincy, Pixie, and now Pretty.

Dogs who shared my love and life were Romeo, Shy Boy, Amy, Aldonza or Al, Savannah, and Mandy.

No matter what point of life I was in, I was always somehow surrounded by animals. In addition to the aforementioned cats and dogs there were dozens of baby field mice Grandpa and I nursed to health after their nests had been uprooted by the mowing of the hay in the field up back of Pleasant View. There were baby chicks and grown roosters and hens, my horse Duke, baby brown bats, birds with injured wings, a garter snake or two, many frogs, newts, a great many goldfish, crayfish, salamanders, and a rather nasty young raccoon Grandpa caught in a trap and had to literally fight before he got the animal calmed and doctored up.

So it was that the menagerie of animals that populated my world was varied—from reptiles, birds, amphibians, and mice to fur-bearing, purring, snuggly creatures who nourished my soul on a constant basis and kept the loneliness at bay.

Looking back I recall that it was Puss who became the first pet of my heart that died suddenly and cruelly on the road in front of our home.

I was about six years of age. The night that Puss met his fate, I was asleep and dreaming of him. He was, as we had found him, a gray-and-white cat with a broad, smiling face and so much love to give. We never knew his origins or anything about his previous owners, but we took him into our hearts quickly and easily. Grandpa adored him and said that he was a real "gentleman cat." Puss was brought into the house to eat his meals (he sometimes favored buttermilk pancakes with syrup as a side dish to his regular cat food) and then released to go outdoors. Grandpa said it was his natural environment and that he kept the mice population in the henhouses down, and that was how he "earned his keep."

Well, in the dream Puss was back on the step in front of the big henhouse up back of Pleasant View—the spot we had found him a few months prior. I approached him slowly and he watched me carefully. However, when I got within a few feet of him he suddenly scampered off and quickly morphed into a "see-through" cat that dashed through the wall of the henhouse and back out again.

I stood in the deep grass outside the henhouse and watched in amazement as he did his vanishing-and-return act several times. My mind briefly registered that this was very unusual behavior for a rather sedate cat, but I sensed no real concern.

On his last pass through and back out, Puss began to glow with a golden light. He meowed a sort of chirpy "meow" and faded from my sight.

The next morning Grandpa came to tell me that Puss had died—hit by a car in front of the house.

I was very sad and cried for a while, missing my furry companion—but then I remembered the dream of him playing a game of hide-and-seek with me, and my young heart was at peace.

I knew that Puss wasn't really lost to me at all.

He had just gone somewhere else for a while, much like the people who had visited me in spirit form.

And I knew that Puss could still play and run and chase mice and be wherever he wanted to be.

I blew my nose and dried my tears and ran outside to help Grandpa get ready for Puss's funeral.

Grandpa got Puss a large cardboard box, and Grandma gave us a big scrap piece of white, soft flannel material with a rose imprint to wrap his broken body in. I put some grass on him and he was buried up back by the side of the big henhouse, where he had loved to catch mice and bask in the sun. After Grandpa and I said a prayer, Grandpa carried me back down the hill and put the shovel in the shed. Then he went to sit with me in his arms on the wall by the steps leading down to the house.

I snuggled against Grandpa's neck.

It was hard to believe that Puss wouldn't be there later to have his cat food and spend time with me before going out to take care of his nightly errands.

Grandpa seemed to understand and was silent—just holding me close and not talking.

It was in the silence of those precious moments in Grandpa's arms that I began to heal and to release Puss to his new life in what I deemed "Kitty Heaven."

Some have said that the return of an animal's spirit shortly after its death is called a "crisis apparition." This is very similar to the type of apparition that sometimes appears to people whose loved one at a distance is passing on. However, even though at least two of my pets appeared to me at the moment of death in dreams, I still hesitate to call it a "crisis apparition." It seems to be better called simply a visit. It causes me to believe in the absolute love link between pet and owner that transcends death.

Having said that, there was an occasion when an animal that was not a pet at all, but rather a creature of the wild whose home was the forest behind Pleasant View, paid an extraordinary after-death visit to my grandmother and me during my sixth year.

It was a very beautiful deer that had been coming on an almost daily basis to the crab apple tree on the bank above the back of the house. This area was and still is clearly visible from the kitchen window. Some nights near twilight when Grandpa was working, Grandma would crouch down and I would stand on my little red wooden chair and watch this delightful creature munch an apple, sniff the air carefully, and return to eating. It was a solitary animal and no others of its kind ever seemed to accompany it.

One morning Grandpa came home from work and said that a deer had been hit by a car in front of the house and was dead. He had pulled it onto the side of the road and said he would have to go to a neighbor's house to use their phone to call the roadmen to come and pick it up.

I knew in my heart that it was the sweet deer Grandma and I had watched enjoying the apples.

Sure enough, a day later when Grandpa was again at work, I stood on my chair with Grandma beside me and we watched out the kitchen window as night fell. We kept the lights off and stood there, both of us hoping that by some miracle it had not been our deer that had been killed.

We waited for a long time. Twilight came and then total darkness fell.

Grandma pulled the shades and turned the light on and both of us knew that our deer was dead.

About a week later, I was again with Grandma in the kitchen and she was about to pull the shades down when she whispered urgently for me to come quickly and get up on my chair but not to make a noise. I did as she asked and then watched in total fascination as a light shadowy shape moved under the crab apple tree. Grandma crouched with her arm around me, and we watched in awe as the shape of a deer seemingly lit with some sort of internal glowing light bent its head to sniff at the apples before vanishing.

Grandma wasn't too fazed by the ghost deer making an appearance. A staunch Southern woman, she had, like Grandpa, seen a few "haunts" as a child in South Carolina. She said that she was "glad" that the deer had come back and that now that it had we probably would never see it again because it had gone on to Heaven. And she was right. I watched out the kitchen window every night for another week after the apparition's appearance, but the animal paid just that one visit that we know of and never again returned.

When Grandpa got home the next day we told him about the deer.

He lifted his cap a couple of times, his way of showing that he was cogitating on the event, and said simply, "Glad it got to Heaven. Hope there are lots of apple trees there for it."

Again, Grandpa's simple acceptance was a balm to my heart.

The appearance of the ghost deer was a memory we shared as a family. We never shared it with anyone else because

Grandpa said, "People don't understand that sort of thing. Best to keep it quiet."

By the time I was in my thirties, many pets had called Pleasant View home, and their all-too-brief presence in my life had brought much joy and renewal to my days.

In 1984, in the aftermath of the car accident and a near-death experience that took me to Heaven, I was able to meet again not only my dear grandparents and many other friends and relatives who were on the other side, but also my beloved pets who had passed on.

This experience was a deeply emotional one that brought me both great sorrow and great joy. Sorrow because I had to leave them all behind to return to the earth plane. Joy because I came away with even more proof that the soul of a pet did indeed survive physical death and live on in soul form. They await our arrival on the other side of life's door as surely as any of our human companions.

That most terrifying of incidents also gave me great comfort indeed. The bonds formed on Earth with my dear pets—those of trust and love—were not broken by death.

For me it was both affirming and magical.

Of the parade of animals that I have loved and who have loved me, cats seem to be the most connected with my psyche.

They are also the ones that return to Pleasant View in spirit shortly after death to reassure me of their continuing presence and love.

The first cat this happened with was my sweet gray tabby cat, Muffin.

Muffin had suffered from intestinal troubles as a kitten, and a local vet saved her from dying because he tried a new surgical procedure on her. She was the total joy of my life, and she and I were very deeply connected on an intense soul level. When she became ill in her later years with feline leukemia I took her to the vet's, where she passed away of the disease.

Muffin's body was brought home and she was buried in the back field next to her dear doggie friend, Al Dog.

It was probably no more than a day after her passing that I went into the kitchen, where her water dish still sat on a mat on the floor and her catnip mouse was lying nearby. I had not wanted to store away her things, as to my mind that would mean giving up hope and having to face the reality of her death.

However, I had no choice.

I bent down to pick up the water dish, and a hint of a very cold breeze went by my hand—followed by the flash of a gray shape that raced past me, past the refrigerator, and into the dining room, where it vanished.

I stood up and at first was totally unaware of what had just happened.

Realization hit me.

I called for Muffin by her pet name, "WeeWeege."

No response.

I thought then that it had all been my imagination and that my sweet little cat really hadn't just run past me, obviously healthy and acting very kittenish. Halfheartedly, I called her name again.

This time I was rewarded by another quick rush of cold air about ankle height and a flash of gray fur as she dashed past me again.

Later that same night I dreamed of Muffin.

She was in a summertime field that had recently been mown.

She approached me slowly from atop the hill and rubbed against my legs and I was able to pet her. I felt the warmth of her body in the sunshine, heard her purrs of contentment beneath my fingers, and felt at peace with the knowledge that she lived on in a healthy and happy state of being in this wide meadow where she could run free and chase birds or butterflies to her heart's content.

I wanted to pick her up and hold her close and kiss her, but she rebuffed my tries to do so, moving away each time I tried.

I kissed my index finger, placed it atop her furry head, looked into her lovely green eyes, and told her I loved her.

She bounded off after a robin that had just landed nearby.

She was, I knew, going to be okay. I also knew that one day we would meet again and be able to renew the bonds of love and togetherness that we had formed while she was in my care during her earthly life.

Other pets of mine deemed it only necessary to appear as a flash of fur in front of me after their passing. Others returned to take up residence for a time in a favorite and familiar sleeping spot.

Al Dog broke loose from her dog house one summer day while I was out in the hills horseback riding. She was hit by a car and died alongside the road a few houses down from Pleasant View.

Again, a companion of my days was gone and I cried endlessly for her.

Al's favorite place to sleep at night was under my bed. She would push and scramble with her claws, making clicking sounds as she moved, until she was fully under, and then she would issue a few soft moans of contentment and fall quickly asleep.

About a week after her passing I was just getting into bed when I felt a very cold rush of air near my feet. I lifted my legs and rubbed my toes. Odd, it was summertime and there was no explanation for the temperature drop so near the floor.

I lay down, pulled up the sheets, and tried to relax.

I missed Al so much. She had been such a comfort and had kept the loneliness at bay especially during the night.

Just as I was about to doze off, I heard a familiar scramble of claws from under the bed and then a very soft doggy moan.

I got up and got onto the floor on my hands and knees and lifted the bed skirt to look under the bed.

I saw nothing, of course, but I knew that somehow Al, like her friend Muffin, had come back to make a visit to reassure me of her continued existence.

I got back into bed and fell asleep quickly because I was reassured that Al was keeping watch even though she was in spirit form.

I began to dream.

Again, the same newly mown sunlit field.

Coming toward me, running joyfully, tongue lolling from her mouth, was my dear Al Dog. She was vibrant and healthy and shone with a splendor that made her fur seem to glimmer golden in the sunbeams.

I got down on my knees and she flew into my arms, licking and wriggling and just bouncing with pure delight at seeing me again.

In the midst of the reunion she suddenly stopped and looked up the hill. A little gray shape materialized from the woods and came racing toward us.

It was Muffin!

Al whined, and Muffin came up and rubbed against her.

They both turned and walked off together and vanished into a golden light.

I awoke and lay very still recalling the dream and the feel of Al's fur and the joy Muffin expressed at seeing her best friend again.

I never again heard the scrabble of Al Dog's feet under my bed but I rested easily, assured by knowing that she and Muffin were frolicking in a beautiful place where we would reunite again when the time was right.

When our dog Mandy became ill with cancer and we knew the end was near, Dan and I were at our wits' end. We had done all we could to make her last hours comfortable, and knowing that she would want to go to Heaven in familiar surroundings Dan carried her up to her bed in the garage and made her comfortable.

I sat with her for a long while, anguished at seeing how the disease had taken her once-firm and sturdy body to a near-twisted, skeletal frame. Yet, as I am not an advocate of putting an animal to sleep, I knew it was the right thing to let her pass at home, in a place she loved.

I sat and held her paw and petted her and talked to her of her favorite places where she had loved to take rides with us: Glimmerglass State Park, where the trails we walked meandered through forest and meadow; alongside the shores of Otsego Lake; and in the fields behind the house where we went daily. I talked, and her brown eyes watched and listened, closing and then reopening as she seemed to let the tales of the joy we had shared enter her soul for remembering.

I was totally exhausted after a while, and for some reason the tiredness was pulling me down.

I kissed Mandy's head, petted her, and told her I'd try to be right back.

In the house I had a quick bite of lunch and then went to lie down for a few minutes. I only wanted to rest for a bit and then get back out to Mandy so that she would not be alone or afraid when the darkness before the light came to her.

I fell across the bed and went into a deep, deep sleep.

Immediately I began to dream.

Before me was a beautiful shining golden staircase that went up, up, up into the clouds. All around the staircase was a shimmery light that seemed lit with a million diamonds.

On the bottom step Mandy was standing and looking back at me. She was still very bent and crippled by the disease that was taking her life.

I looked up at the many steps and wondered if she had the strength to make it all the way to the top.

She whined and went up another step and looked back at me again.

For some reason I was torn between wanting to urge her to go to the top of the stairs and to keep her at the bottom with me.

She whined again, this time with insistence in her tone.

It took all my courage, but I knew what I had to do.

"Go on, puppy!" I told her mentally. "It's okay. Go on! You'll be okay. Daddy and I will see you again one day."

She rushed back to me, and I could plainly see that in the few moments that she had stood on the stairway she had youthened and was now looking more like her healthy and vibrant self. Gone was the twisted body ravaged with illness—she was almost a puppy again, eager to play and cavort about. I hugged her oh-so-tightly, and when she began to squirm in my grasp I knew the time had now come to let her go. She ran off, went up several steps, looked back at me once more, then bounded up all the steps taking them two or more at a time. She got to the top, where the golden clouds enveloped her and she was gone from my sight.

I woke up when Dan came into the bedroom and quietly told me with tears streaming down his face that Mandy had just died.

Mandy's best friend was our sweet boy cat, Pixie. At one time topping the scales at twenty pounds, Pixie was one of five kittens who, along with his mother, we had rescued from behind a neighbor's hedge. Pixie was actually the runt of the litter, and because he couldn't nurse I eventually had to feed him with a medicine dropper with warmed-up evaporated milk in it. He thrived, and when it came time to find homes for his brothers, sisters, and his mother, Dan and I decided to keep him.

It was a choice we never regretted.

Pixie was just a lover and a marvelously smart cat. He even learned how to "kiss" me by gently putting his mouth to my lips, and he especially loved just to cuddle and cuddle endlessly with either Dan or me when we watched television at night.

Sweet Pixie became ill with renal failure and died a few months later at the vet's, despite all our attempts to save him. I truly thought that he would pull through, as our little girl cat, Quincy, had had the same illness and recovered to full health. The loss of Pixie was the second crushing loss of a pet in less than a year and a half.

I always thought that Pixie gave up after the death of his Mandy Dog and mourned her on a deeper level than we realized.

And on a soul level I felt that I had failed Pixie by letting him die at the vet's in a cage. I believe that all my pets, if possible, should pass at home surrounded by love and the familiar sights and sounds and smells that had been a part of their lives.

Shortly after Pixie's passing I was walking into the bedroom, and suddenly a whisk of very cold air swirled around my ankles and a quick image of white-and-black fur dashed past me and ran out the bedroom door and into the dining room. I followed, hoping to catch a glimpse of my sweet boy. I waited. A few minutes later, there was the rush of cold air, as the white-and-black fur shadow made a beeline under the dining room table—the place where Mandy had lain down on her blanket when she had come in for the evening, and the place where Pixie also took up residence when she was in the house.

I reasoned that Pixie, now free of his burdensome earthly body, was searching for his Mandy Dog in the place where he remembered her to be.

About a week after this incident I dreamed of them.

Here once more was the sunlit meadow.

The sun was shining down warm and golden, the grass was emerald green and soft beneath my sandaled feet, and the birds flew past, their wings flickering through the air with gentle swishes.

I turned and looked up the hill and shaded my eyes.

From out of the far corner of the field, where the Pleasant View pets rest in their graves beneath the shade of several trees, two shapes formed.

Before I could react, Mandy Dog came bounding down the hill with Pixie running beside her, keeping perfect pace. The two seemed unaware of my presence. They ran and played, with Mandy bending down with her rear in the air, her face alight with joy, and Pixie batting at her nose as he had always done.

I felt as though I were being given a special glimpse of a friendship between two animals that extended beyond time and space, one that death could not sever—much like Al Dog and Muffin.

The two animals continued to play, and then suddenly took off and ran up the hill and into the forest and vanished.

Their joy at being reunited was so beautiful, and I was truly at peace as I turned from the meadow and awoke.

Quincy was a sweet black-and-white girl cat that I first fell in love with sight unseen after our sweet gray Persian cat, Brutus, passed away of feline leukemia. Pleasant View had been horribly catless for about a year, and I had tried my best to hold out and not get attached to another feline because I dreaded the pain of saying goodbye. However, one day in the autumn of 1990 I happened to scan the local newspaper's want ads and saw an ad in the "Free" column—"A Sweet Female Cat" to a good home. Intrigued, I called the number immediately, and the next morning the owner brought me my baby girl cat. She informed me that Quincy had been named after Quincy, Massachusetts, as Quincy the cat was born during a time when the woman's daughter had been to a hospital in that city.

From the moment she arrived at our home Quincy was a spitfire with an amazing agility and a good bit of chutzpah. At first she was barricaded in the kitchen with a piece of plywood to keep her contained. She would have none of that! Though only about three months old, she easily scaled the barrier and ran about the house at night, chasing the light beams of the cars that passed by on Route 7 and consequently ripping off most of the wallpaper on the dining room walls.

Her personality was totally intact at a young age, and she made it known quite early on that she was not a cuddling cat at all. She squirmed and fought to be loose and was not against giving you a quick scratch on the hand if you tried to keep her captive for some hugs.

When Quincy was about twelve she developed kidney failure. She dropped in weight to about three pounds and spent a week or so at the vet's. Dan and I went as often as we could to visit her and snuggle her in towels and fuzzy blankets with the scent of home on them. When she was at last allowed to come home with us, she had to have sub-cutaneous fluids given to her, and a most frightening arena of care opened up for Dan and me. I didn't like pushing the huge needle into her scruff, and she didn't care too much for it either.

Finally, about a week later I decided on a new tack and stopped the fluids. I told her that if she wanted to heal and stay with us, it was now up to her. I began to warm up her cat food and make certain there was lots of juice from the can on the plate. Then I would sit beside her bed near the kitchen chimney and feed her, first with a small spoon and then she began to eat on her own. Her tenacity and desire to live was incredible. Two weeks later she was up and about— a bit unsteady on her feet, but rushing through the house and going to lie down on her warm towel on the bedroom win-dowsill. She was drinking and eating on her own and using the litter as if nothing at all had happened to her. She was truly a miracle of a cat, and I so honored and respected her for the amazing animal she was.

Petite and strong-willed, Quincy would stay with us for almost nine more years.

She passed away wrapped in a warm towel in her favorite cardboard-box snuggy bed by the kitchen stove on January 1, 2010. She was almost twenty-one years old, which translates to almost one-hundred and forty human years!

I was with her to the end, watching as life slowly left her small frame. Her paws reached out to me, and I held them in my hand, breaking down and thanking her for being my cat. She looked up at me with eyes that were already gazing at another dimension I could not see. Thankfully her passing was peaceful, and she seemed to make the transition calmly and easily.

Quincy was buried that winter day next to her friends Pixie and Mandy Dog.

The next day she was back in spirit, rushing about the rooms between the kitchen and the dining room and vanishing down the hallway to the bedroom. Dan and I saw her on many occasions—a petite cat streaking past us with her white-and-black fur blending into the shadows and the sun.

Two weeks after she passed she came to me in a dream.

Again I was in the familiar summer meadow with the sun shining down full and warm. Quincy came as if out of the sun's rays, and she was now younger and healthier. She looked exactly as she had when she had been in her prime and before her kidney problems.

Just as she had lived, Quincy was on the run, rushing toward her goals and oblivious to whatever else might be happening.

She came toward me as if out of nowhere, dancing sideways, giving me a quick look, and rushing up the hill with Pixie and Mandy close behind.

I woke up and knew that she was fine now and totally enjoying the feeling of freedom allowed by her new spirit body.

An afternote on Quincy: she did not return to me in a dream again, but rather this past December when I was ill in bed. There was no mistaking her smooth purr and the quick patter of her little feet on the mattress as she rushed past to lie on the pillows where she had napped with me so often when she was alive.

I was most grateful for her presence, and it was one of the many things that helped me heal.

Despite the debate that continues about the survival of animal souls, I know in my heart that beloved pets are blessed with innocent souls that carry intelligence and many of the better human traits of love, compassion, and kindness with them from this world into the hereafter. They are blessings in our lives, both on the earth plane and from the spirit world, and death does not separate them from us.

They are our companions in spirit and eagerly await being reunited with us when our time comes to leave here.

Afterword

One of the absolutely most comforting things I do know about the dead and that I find solace in is this: those who loved us in life are still very concerned about us after they die. My dear grandmother still finds ways to visit me in spirit whenever I am ill or hurting physically or emotionally. Whenever I am afraid or want to cry out with pain, there is my grandmother's familiar scent of Cashmere Bouquet powder filling the room. Then the feel of the side of the bed sinking down a bit, as if someone had just sat down, and a cool breeze soothes me into dreamland.

Likewise, my dear and departed pets come to visit me during my healing times. My spirit cats simply announce themselves with a quick run and jump on the bed or sofa. There is a skitter of paws and a quick sinking of the mattress or cushions, the comforting and swift sound of a purr, or the brush of soft fur against my face or legs. I relax into their love and thank them for their concern and the constant care they bring to me from Heaven.

Over the time I have spent in communication with the dead I have learned many lessons and have also been left with just as many questions.

Grandpa was very right when he told me that death was just a going to sleep in one place and waking up in another. Butch was also right when he told me that one had to trust the process and do a free-fall into the experience. All the dead I have met, whether they died in their sleep, of a disease, or in a tragic accident, seem to become at peace with their situation. Most seem to need to rest after the transition from life to death. Some, like my grandfather, seem to alternate between the idyllic world of reunion with family while continuing a sort of spiritual learning spiral upward—almost as if certain lessons had to be learned on the other side before progression to the next level of life could be attained.

Others seem stuck for a while, neither moving forward nor backward. Some don't seem to move at all and stay put in the places they loved in life, surrounding themselves with the souls of those they knew and trusted, living out their daily ventures with no remarkable change at all. They cook and clean, chase hummingbirds through flower gardens, continue with projects they didn't get to complete, migrate between the dimensions of Earth and Heaven, and seem perfectly content to do so. They maintain the personalities they had in life and don't really make many new acquaintances but tend to stay with the tried and true friendships they forged on Earth.

There are souls like Beverly, who refuse to leave their gravesite, and others like Jeremy, who roam far and wide and are able to change their attire to match the day. Others never change one piece of the clothing that they were either buried or cremated in.

Some prefer to visit in dreams and spend a long time in interacting and conversing. Others don't feel so inclined and only send the briefest of mental shouts to me in hopes that I may be the one who will deliver their message to a loved one. From these I have found that the dead don't really care if you are labeled as "crazy" if you deliver a message from them to another living being. They simply have found a receptive person and decided to open a frequency and attempt to urge that the message be given. If it isn't I have never gotten the impression that they are too concerned. They will simply find someone else who will or await the arrival of the person on the other side.

Thankfully, all of my interactions with the dead have been, except for that one instance with the nasty old woman, full of respect, love, and mutual trust. Most, if not all, are totally cognizant of the fact of their passing and some, like Irene, are momentarily angered by the fact that their final wishes were not carried out but quickly find their way to acceptance. Others don't seem to care at all and are glad to be free of the physical body, especially if it was ill or badly injured. I see this also with the pet spirits that have come to me in dreams. They, like many of their human counterparts who have passed, are younger, healthier, and full of vibrant energy. They run and play and cavort and spend each moment in joy—they are perfectly content to be in spirit and seem to harmonize with the afterlife.

My near-death experiences have taken me through the void that divides the living from the dead, and there, as I've noted, are marvelous vistas—grand and peaceful and full of light. There is no more division among the races, colors, or creeds—there is only love and a togetherness based on mutual understanding of having gone through the turmoil of earthly life and somehow finding the way back again to the true *home*.

From the dead I have learned so many things.

I have learned the preciousness of life. At any moment for anyone alive now on this planet the balance held for each of us in the wallet of time that we are given at birth can run out. It can run out for humans and pets. There are no guarantees whatsoever. I know through my own near-death experiences that this is so. As a young girl dying of pneumonia, death was only a handclasp away. As a teenager dying in my bed of an asthma attack and being saved by divine intervention, I learned that despite the nearness of loved ones, death can sneak in and take you quickly. As an adult in a near-fatal car crash wherein I was given my glimpse of Heaven and returned with a clear mission and incredible knowledge, I learned the lesson of my mortality. In each occurrence it took only the space of a heartbeat to step from this world into the next.

From the dead I have learned to care deeply. The spirits I have visited and who have taken the immense amount of energy and time to come to me are extremely caring, loving, and still deeply concerned about my well-being despite their being in non-physical form. Love doesn't end with death—in fact, I now know that it intensifies. Love expands on the other side and all negative emotions such as jealousy, fear, anger—all these and more are eradicated, and all the inhabitants of that beautiful realm it has been my privilege to know are filled with joy and peace. From their beings shines a light that encompasses and heals.

The dead never feign love—none of the ones I met have. They are very serious about honesty of emotions and not having conditions attached to loving. It's as if they've passed through some sort of love veil that gives them incredible experience and heightens their sense of compassion, sympathy, and empathy for one another as well as for those they love who are still earthbound. Their sympathy level is amped up to the highest intensity. They are ultra-concerned about the effects they will have on humans and tread carefully when initiating a visit in form or dreams.

Of course, again, I can only speak of the dead I have met who are the kindly ones. There are others who have passed over who are probably just as querulous as they were on Earth, but then I believe that even they eventually learn to love fully. Those who have passed maintain their earthly personalities to a degree. If they believed in a particular doctrine on Earth, they will believe it on the other side. Many will retain all their likes, dislikes, prejudices, and opinions. It's just that the attachments to negative earthly feelings seem to eventually fall away as acceptance fills the void.

After death there is a knowledge that is deep and at last comprehends what the soul's life mission was about. I have heard it said again and again that each one of us is a miracle and that we are put here on Earth to express miracles in our lives and in the lives of others. And I believe and know this to be true. We do all have a mission. Many are sent here to Earth with only the scantest of clues as to what that mission might be. Some are lucky and arrive with a knowing that is beyond incredible. Others have either to come upon their life mission by accident or seek it out with help from others.

I have always been thankful that I knew by age three that I wanted to be a writer. The desire to do this creative work burned in my soul as soon as I could put letters together to form words. By age four I had written my very first extremely short, short story. And I do mean extremely short. It was called "The Little Hurt Bird," and it was about four sentences long. It told the true story of a baby robin that fell from its nest in a tree on our front lawn and hurt its leg. My grandpa, as wise in the ways of birds as he was all living things, explained to me that usually we would have to leave the bird to the care of its mother, who was most likely around somewhere watching the whole scene carefully. He told me to never, ever pick up a baby bird that had fallen from the nest if it seemed able to move around all right. But with this particular bird's leg being injured, the mother bird would not be able to help. So Grandpa got a small box, pulled lots of grass with my help, got a dish of water, and then set the bird's leg with small pieces of sticks and tape.

I helped him by soothing the scared little creature; the poor thing looked up at us and shivered a lot but didn't, as Grandpa had worried, "die with fear." A sturdy little thing, the robin took up residence in its box next to my bed. Grandpa sent me out with my little red shovel and blue plastic bucket to dig for worms along the edge of the garden where the soil was already tilled. These worms had to be mashed up and pushed down the bird's throat very carefully.

With all this love and care the baby bird flourished, its leg healed, and one day we released it up back in our field. It had been trying to fly in the house, and we had placed a screen atop the box. My first short story about that bird was deeply praised by my grandparents when I read it to them—and because of their belief in my skills I was on my life path.

So from Grandpa, and later the dead, I learned about life missions and the sacredness of them. I learned that beyond what we do for a job or to make a living there is a much grander scheme that we are to fit into, and that it is something that takes us outside ourselves and helps to make the world a better place. Grandpa, far ahead of his time, told me when I was looking into colleges for the study of secretarial skills that the education I would receive would get me a good job with which I would be able to earn money and take care of myself and any family I might have. But he admonished me that my *real job* on Earth would be something totally different from "just being a worker."

"Find what you love to do and share it with others," he said to me during my searching teenage years. Then, as Grandpa said, when you leave this world you will know that you made it better for your having been here.

So the dead instructed, and I have listened with all my heart ever since I was a little girl.

The seasons turned over onto one another, and light and shadows came into my life and left and returned again.

I believe that it was after Jeremy's death that I began to really understand the true meaning of acceptance and forgiveness.

Because another thing the dead come to understand and try to impart to the living is real forgiveness.

In paradise there is no animosity.

There is no jealousy or hate or dislike or lying or stealing or backstabbing or gossip.

Or at least I have never witnessed it.

All are one and united in joy. There are no more care-worn days, no more bills to pay, no more trying to one-up the other person—it is all over, and thus there is no reason for any ill feelings.

And, after all this, what of the fear of dying when our time comes to leave the earthly plane behind? Will it be painful and scary?

Perhaps a little, and only then I believe because we fear leaving behind those earthly attachments to family, friends, pets, places, and possessions that we have formed. We fear that we will not see the faces of our beloved ones or ever be held in loving arms or have a favorite dog or cat by our side.

Again my experiences have taught me that this is not so.

The bonds formed on Earth are never broken but are only made stronger on the other side. There is reunion and there is health and peace and joy that is beyond incredible.

There is to me no greater consolation than to know that those who have passed on and I have loved and who have loved me, be they human or animal, are truly only a heartbeat away.

Those beloved ones will come swiftly whenever we are sick or lonely or lost. We might not be able to see them with our eyes, but if we listen with our hearts we will know they are nearby offering support, hope, compassion, and love, and that when we see them again in paradise we will find that this life was only a prelude to the next glorious one awaiting us on the other side of death's door.

THE END—Or is it?

To Write to the Author

If you wish to contact the author or would like more information about this book, please write to the author in care of Llewellyn Worldwide Ltd. and we will forward your request. Both the author and publisher appreciate hearing from you and learning of your enjoyment of this book and how it has helped you. Llewellyn Worldwide Ltd. cannot guarantee that every letter written to the author can be answered, but all will be forwarded. Please write to:

Marilou Trask-Curtin
℅ Llewellyn Worldwide
2143 Wooddale Drive
Woodbury, MN 55125-2989

Please enclose a self-addressed stamped envelope for reply, or $1.00 to cover costs. If outside the USA, enclose an international postal reply coupon.

Bridge to the
Afterlife
A Medium's Message of Hope & Healing

"*Bridge to the Afterlife* is a remarkable story
of spirit's survival. Troy's message will stir your
soul and remind you that your loved ones
are always with you."
—**John Holland**, psychic medium and author of *Born Knowing*

TROY PARKINSON

Bridge to the Afterlife

A Medium's Message of Hope & Healing

TROY PARKINSON

What if you could talk to the Other Side? What would you say? And what messages would the spirits have for you?

Spiritual medium Troy Parkinson, a rising star in the paranormal world, shares fascinating firsthand stories of his communications with the spirit realm.

Channeling spirits was the last thing Troy Parkinson ever thought he'd do. A North Dakota native and self-described "ordinary guy," he first attended a spiritualist meeting when he was a college student. After receiving a message that night from his grandmother's spirit, he decided to pursue mediumship training through the world-renowned First Spiritual Temple in Boston.

He now travels around the country, doing readings for large audiences and presenting workshops that teach people how to develop their own spirit-communication abilities. Troy's moving story and amazing messages from spirit will touch your heart, inspire your soul, and remind you that your loved ones are always with you.

978-0-7387-1435-6, 240 pp., 6 x 9 **$15.95**

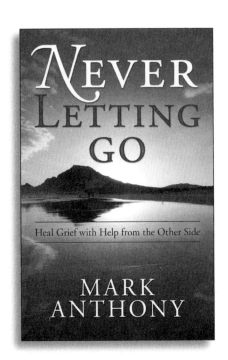

NEVER LETTING GO

Heal Grief with Help from the Other Side

MARK ANTHONY

Never Letting Go

Heal Grief with Help from the Other Side

MARK ANTHONY

After his mother's death, Mark Anthony was devastated—until he experienced the impossible: a visit from her. This profound and life-changing experience not only helped him cope with crushing grief but also inspired him to develop his gift of spirit communication and bring healing to others.

Opening up to the notion that life transcends death is the first powerful lesson in this engaging and uplifting guide to healing from grief. Evidence of the soul's immortality is illustrated in moving accounts of the author delivering life-affirming messages of forgiveness, gratitude, hope, and comfort from loved ones on the Other Side. By sharing his experiences and wisdom as a psychic lawyer and medium, Mark Anthony reveals the healing nature of spirit communication and the rewards of opening our hearts to beloved friends and family in spirit.

978-0-7387-2721-9, 288 pp., 5³⁄₁₆ x 8   **$15.95**

To order, call 1-877-NEW-WRLD
Prices subject to change without notice
Order at Llewellyn.com 24 hours a day, 7 days a week!

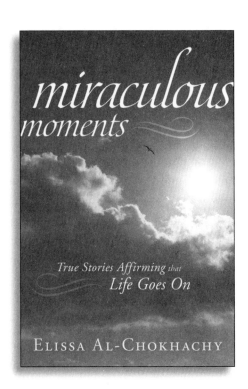

miraculous moments

moments

True Stories Affirming that
Life Goes On

ELISSA AL-CHOKHACHY

Miraculous Moments
True Stories Affirming that Life Goes On
ELISSA AL-CHOKHACHY

Does life go on after death? Will we ever be reunited with loved ones? Does love ever die?

Heartfelt testimony to the everlasting human spirit can be found in this wondrous collection of true stories from people who have seen, heard, and felt love from beyond. Laugh along with the husband who enjoys one last April Fools joke from his deceased wife. Rejoice with the family who are reassured by the presence of the father and husband whose life was lost on September 11, 2001.

Told with courage and warmth, these vivid accounts— hugs from family members who have passed, sightings of souls leaving a body at the time of death, encounters with angels, near-death experiences, and even visits from the spirits of beloved pets—offer hope, reassurance, and comfort to anyone who is mourning a lost loved one or has ever wondered about life after death.

978-0-7387-2122-4, 312 pp., 6 x 9   **$17.95**

PATRICK MATHEWS

NEVER SAY
GOODBYE

A Medium's Stories of
Connecting with Your Loved Ones